Praise for **RISE ABO**

MW01275196

'This book will stretch your mind to a degree you've not yet imagined. I have been a serious student of great books and authors for over 57 years and I would consider this book to be among the best. Denise Beaupré is an insightful leader and her book *RISE ABOVE* will provide you with the tools you require to live the life of your dreams."

~ Bob Proctor, Master Success Coach, Teacher in *The Secret*

"Inspired, motivated and ready to make the change! Denise's passion and true desire to see everyone achieve their best life will inspire and motivate you to lead the life you've always dreamed of. If you are ready to make the change, you need to read this book. You won't put it down until you're on your way to Rising Above!"

~ Kelly Henderson, CEO, KelKat & Associates

"*RISE ABOVE* will help you jump start your life. Denise Beaupré teaches you how to take charge of your life and forge a path. Whether you are looking for more abundance in your personal or business life, there are tools for everyone.

This is a must read for anyone looking to step into a leadership role and a great reminder for those of us already in leadership roles. You alone are responsible for where you are now and where you end up. Denise inspires us to become a better version of ourselves."

~ Deanna Parker, Former Adult Educator and Business Owner

"An absolutely great book that shows us how approaching every day with a positive attitude, appreciation and determination will lead to success. I enjoyed reading it and think you will too."

~ Joe Palmer, Senior Vice President, Palmer Atlantic

"I am feeling so pumped-up right now!!! OMG Denise Beaupré gave me so many creative ideas in *RISE ABOVE* on how to improve my experiences with my clients and how to motivate them to share their personal experiences with others to create referrals. Thank you to Denise for sharing!"

~ Pamela Cail, Rainbow Energy Alive

"Embrace this book! It is a truly useful guide to help you be the best you can be. Do not accept or permit mediocre. *RISE ABOVE* will be enormously helpful to those facing personal and professional challenges or to just be a better version of yourself! A wonderful combination of idealism and realism."

~ Kim Richardson, President, TransRep Inc.

"This book is pure gold! Not just another book on leadership, it is a simple and extremely impactful understanding of what a true leader is and how to incorporate leadership into your life and in your work."

~ Arash Vossoughi, Proctor Gallagher Institute

RISE
ABOVE

Create the abundant life you desire

DENISE BEAUPRÉ

Published by
Hasmark Publishing
www.hasmarkpublishing.com

Disclaimer

Permission should be addressed in writing to Denise Beaupré at
info@deniseBeaupré.com

Editor: Sigrid Macdonald
Book Magic
http://bookmagic.ca

Cover and Book Design: Anne Karklins
annekarklins@gmail.com

Photography: Denis Duquette.ca

ISBN 13: 978-1-989161-37-1
ISBN 10: 1989161375

To my current staff at Auction Transport and my husband,
I aim to be a better version of myself each and every day
because you all give me the best of yourselves each and every day.
Best of the best, cream of the crop!

TABLE OF CONTENTS

FOREWORD

There is a great quote that goes like this: "by their fruits you will know them". Quite simply, when you look at someone's results, you will know the person.

If you want to know what someone is like, look at their results. Why do I mention that? Because Denise Beaupré is a woman who has created phenomenal results. It is obvious to me that she has a healthy attitude about life. She knows how to create success. She knows how to rise above the rest and she continues to do so. What does that mean to you? If you are looking to improve your results, you are in the right place.

For many years now, I have worked with authors helping them to write their books, make them international best sellers and create a profitable revenue producing business following their passion. Many of these authors have a fabulous understanding of the laws of the universe, but seldom have they created extraordinary success.

Understanding what it takes to succeed is only part of the process. And, although it is an important part of the process, real results come from the application of these wise thoughts.

The one thing that I love about this book, **Rise Above**, is that Denise is providing a very simple, easy to understand foundation and tops it off with practical application. You can follow this book and her guidance and begin at once to improve and increase your results, if that is what you desire to do.

What makes this book unique is the no-nonsense approach Denise takes. She is not holding back on strong recommendations and her intense beliefs. She is obviously very passionate about this subject because year after year after year, she continues to improve her own results.

Before you begin reading this book, I invite you to really think about what you want. Really think about it. What would you love? What would you love to experience in your life? What would you love to do? Where do you want to go? Whom do you choose to become? What accomplishments would you love to attain? How much money would you love to earn? What about your relationships… business/career goals… health… contribution to society? Put some thought into what you would love for all areas of your life… and really THINK.

Simple questions, right? Well, so few people invest any time whatsoever to put any conscious thought to these important questions. I suggest you start there, because when you know what you want, Denise Beaupré can help you get it.

The fact that you are holding this book in your hand is a demonstration that you have a desire to improve your results. I can confidently say you are in the right place. Set some time aside now and begin to study this book. Have this book become an important part of your daily study practice. Implement the ideas that Denise recommends and then watch your results soar. I am grateful Denise decided to write her book as I know it will help people all over the world. Maybe you are one of them. I am also confident that Denise would love to hear about your success too; therefore, plan to send her an update once you implement the strategies in **Rise Above** and share with her your own success.

Wishing you great success.

Peggy McColl
New York Times Best Selling Author

PART ONE

INTRODUCTION

Abundant Life

Do you have the courage to live the life you really want? Do you feel worthy of being successful and happy? Do you allow yourself to live a life most people don't understand? Do you find yourself wanting more of something different? More passion perhaps, more freedom, money, romance, love? Or do you constantly worry about what other people may think? Do you assume that you are stuck with the way things are? Or better yet, do you think you can't have everything?

An abundant life comes from a creative mind, which means coming from a place of originality, using your mind to come up with ways to make your life better than what you currently have. It comes to those who choose to aim high, which could be explained as having high expectations and not letting anyone convince you otherwise. I believe it also comes from rising above anything that's thrown at you, such as obstacles, rejection, ridicule, depression, judgment, drama, gossip, dis-ease and so on.

Prosperity and success do not come from luck. They come from your attitude toward life in general in the same manner as suffering, bad luck and dis-ease come from your attitude. Some people think that they are undeserving of an abundant life. Unfortunately, they will remain undeserving until they change their attitude toward prosperity and success. Suffering, poverty and worry are all about choices just as an abundant life is.

I don't believe that anyone was brought into this world to suffer in any way. What I do believe is that each one of us has a different belief or outlook on what living a life of abundance means. Does it mean having lots of money? Or does it mean living a life full of joy? I can't answer that question for you because the answer is unique to you. One thing I can tell you is that it certainly does not mean an abundance of bad luck or an abundance of stress. We have every right to allow positive abundance in our lives. In fact, we should expect it. We should live with love and lots of it, we should be healthy and we should be successful.

Beliefs are simply a way of thinking; that's all they are. Change your way of thinking and you alter your results. The average person is brought up in a ridiculous world of judgment, ridicule and peer pressure. Judgment, ridicule and peer pressure are hurtful to humankind and stop us from wanting good for ourselves. We were judged if we believed in something greater than the neighbor next door believed. Judged for being happy, judged for being successful and so on. It takes a lot of self-talk and self-discipline to reject those negative thoughts and to believe in things that are not yet a reality. You know the saying, "I'll believe it when I see it"? How many times have we heard that? I'm here to help you change that way of thinking. I want you to think the opposite way. Believe in the magic, in the unseen as if you already have it and living your dreams. You want true success in your life on a personal level, your health or your finances? Then you need to train your mind, which is your biggest asset, to think differently and go against what you have already learned at a very young age.

If you are holding this book in your hands, it's either because you went looking for it or it was given to you. Either way, it's no mistake that this book has found you as well. I can help you find your way to success and to rise above all judgment, ridicule, peer pressure or even self-sabotage that you've ever encountered in your life up until now. I believe by rising above you will become your best self and it will reflect in everything you do. This book showed up in your life because your subconscious mind has been looking for it. You've attracted it into your life just like everything else you are living at this moment in time, be it negative or positive. And now you are ready to RISE ABOVE it all.

You may or may not know me on a personal level and that's okay. I want to explain that I live my life every day with the mentality of always doing the right thing. Being ethical and coming from a place of integrity for me is of the utmost importance. I speak the truth and it may be difficult to hear at times. I know I find it difficult when someone tells me the harsh truth about myself. It's never fun and sometimes, it takes me a while to get over it. I might cry, or yell or just go into my little cocoon because I'm embarrassed, but once I'm done pitying myself, I use the feedback that was given to me to better myself going forward. I can honestly say that the reason I am successful today is because of just that: being honest, ethical and coming from integrity. When I look to a friend for advice, I want the truth and I can always tell when that person is not being honest with me. Anyone who has ever engaged in a conversation with me or looked for advice rarely hears what they think they want to hear. How would that be of any help to you if I only said what you wanted to hear? You can't grow as a human being that way.

I could probably give you many examples of what I mean, but I'll start with one. My background was in real estate and if you know any Realtors, you know that it's a tough business. You need to be out marketing yourself, you need to talk to people and you need to get up in the morning. You should be taking all the courses you can and you have to work very long hours. Many Realtors have a difficult time with this and when the sales are not what they were hoping for, they get discouraged, feel sorry for themselves and start blaming everything and everyone around them. Their broker is the worst broker in town or the market is crap. The interest rates are just too high and so on. In my 13 years in real estate, I was engaged in many of those conversations and it's so easy to get caught up in this mentality.

If you were sitting in front of me complaining about your life or your finances not being what you want them to be, I would be asking you these questions:

What time do you get up in the morning?

Do you market yourself?

Do you have a website?

Are you *really* doing what you should be doing?

Or are you too busy worrying about what can go wrong?

And then I'd be telling you that your broker, the market or your boss has nothing to do with your results. It all starts with you! Get up at a decent time, write your affirmations, attend trainings, read a book and attack the day. The difference between successful people and not so successful people is that successful people do what other people don't want to do. They also get over their sad moments or hurt egos much quicker than the average person. They get upset, they get frustrated, they get hurt just like everyone else, but the difference with successful people is that they can easily shake it off in five minutes while others will take five hours, five months or five years.

It makes no difference if you are still in school, a stay-at-home mom, just starting in your career, running your own business or an executive in the corporate world – this book will help everyone. I, like you, had to start somewhere. No one is born successful or an expert at anything. As a young woman fresh out of high school, I left my parents' home when I was 18 years old. I visualized from a young age being out on my own and growing up to be a successful woman. I didn't have a clue how I would make it happen, but I was determined. I had to leave home to go to university. I lived in a small community with a population of maybe 2500 at the time. If I wanted to pursue my education, I had no choice but to leave. I made the decision that I would never return to my hometown or to my parents' house other than for visiting on special occasions.

I made the decision to do whatever I could to support myself and I did just that. Luckily, my parents were still supportive and helped me achieve this. They assisted me financially whenever I needed them, but I did everything I could not to have to ask them for any help. My first summer job away from home was seven miles away from where my new home was. I had no car and no money for taxis. We didn't have Uber then. Trust me; life has changed. So, I chose to take my mountain bike and pedal my way to work every day. I was in the best shape of my life that summer due to the 14-mile return trip from work. You see, I was determined to do what others didn't want to do. I was determined to make it on my own and work hard at whatever I had to do. Fast forward to now and I've learned that I can work hard and long hours to achieve success, but I can also do certain things in a certain way that will bring on even bigger success simply by using all my faculties. I can think smarter and create the life I want.

I never received any degrees from university. In fact, I'm what you would call a "dropout" from my post-secondary education. I hated school. I would go to my classes, lay my head on my desk and fall asleep. I don't recommend you follow in my footsteps as school is important, but when I think back, I realize I was bored. I wanted to be out there in the world. I wanted to experience life and learn everything I could in this crazy, fast-changing world we live in. I always managed to get work. I was never fired from any job. Actually, I received bonuses on many occasions. I always did the best I could because that's what I knew from an early age.

My parents owned a gas station when I was growing up and I worked for them from the age of 14 years old. I pumped gas, I worked the cash register and I changed tires with my father and watched him do all sorts of mechanic work. My mother was the bookkeeper while doing a lot of volunteer work and raising four girls. When I was just 15, my mother had to have major surgery, which meant she would not be able to do the books for the garage. She showed me how to do the accounting, by hand, I must add, because back then, computers did not exist. I was in charge of finances for the family business at the tender age of 15. I honestly don't know too many people who have had that same opportunity growing up. I never knew that all those experiences would make me into the successful woman I am today. My parents probably didn't know either, but I give them much credit for who I have become.

I was bored in school and at work; I was always searching for something bigger and better. My first big job was in the insurance industry. I started in the call center and made my way to the sales support position. I was always dreaming of my future. I thought that becoming a salesperson in the insurance industry would be a good fit for me. My dream stopped when one of my superiors told me that I would never be promoted because I was missing certain body parts: "male body parts," to be exact. In today's world, comments like that would probably result in official complaints to HR; however, in those days, women just didn't speak up. At that moment, I could have accepted that man's response and continued working there as an underling, but I knew he was wrong and I was determined to show the world what I was made of even if I didn't know what that was. I am so grateful that I was smart enough to walk away from that sort of environment, from belittlement and stigma toward woman.

The experience and lessons that I will share with you here come from mostly my background in real estate and the trucking world: hands-on experience with sales, marketing, customer service, people, employees, finance and personal growth. I've encountered many speed bumps along the way just as most people do in life and there were many days where I could have given up. Today, I still experience speed bumps, but I'm now able to master challenges that come my way and deal with them differently. If I feel like giving up, I step away for a bit, recharge and get right back on track.

All successful people will tell you that they go through daily obstacles. It's part of life! This book will help you accept these diversions for what they are and to be a success in life, no matter what. You may not have the same background as I do, but that makes no difference. I'm here to show you that the industry you are in changes nothing. Look at me: I went from being a successful Realtor to running a trucking business. I had years where I sold 80 to 100 houses. I made more money than most doctors and lawyers make in the city I live in. I had all the awards you can imagine and I made the firm's list of top 100 Realtors in North America for four consecutive years. My name was a household name and my face was on billboards all over the city; I was helping people make the biggest purchase of their lives and I was making good money. What else could I want?

I remember being at a real estate convention in Nashville many years ago. One evening, I found myself among my peers sharing stories and I will never forget the words that came out of my mouth. I said, "there's more to me than real estate". I surprised myself when I said it because I had no idea where those words came from. Even then, I knew life had more to offer. I knew I was capable beyond measures.

I truly loved real estate and I equally hated it with a passion. I'll be sharing these stories with you along the way. One day, while driving down the highway after showing houses to clients, I don't know what came over me, but I remember saying to myself, "what are you doing, Denise? Your husband needs you in the trucking business. You need to be there to help him." Talk about getting out of your comfort zone. The one thing I was good at and successful at, yet I was willing to give it all up at that moment. Why? I didn't know why at the time, but it didn't matter. I just knew I had to do it.

What followed my decision was not at all what I thought would happen and I was faced with many surprises and adversity, but I chose to keep going. Frustrations and fear of failure are all part of the game. I made a complete 360 in my career and it changed my life to this day. I went from working out of my car selling houses – I only had myself and one assistant to worry about – to dealing with million-dollar contracts, having over 20 employees to look after and making sure I could feed their families every week and I don't regret any of it. I never looked back and that's exactly what you need to do: decide and never look back!

I know that the reason I feel as though I'm always meant to do more is because I have goals and big ones at that. I accomplish one goal and I create a new one. Even though my husband and I now have a successful trucking business, we continue to dream bigger. We went many years without any sort of profit of barely any money in our bank account, but we always chose to consciously look at ourselves as successful individuals. Day after day, year after year, we achieved and still achieve new milestones and bigger goals.

Everything I do, everyone I meet, all my interactions with employees and customers, all come into play. I work on myself every day through self-talk and self-discipline. I know this book found its way to you because you want to RISE ABOVE like I do or maybe this book is to help you recognize it in someone else and to share the book with that special person, so they can RISE ABOVE ALL.

This book is meant to help you grow as an individual or a business-person. I will show you how to stay strong and how to implement tactics in your everyday dealings, so you can grow, help others grow, help yourself get a higher position in your current job or make a quantum leap in your business. I believe that business is just that, business. It doesn't matter what industry you come from. In fact, I believe that with my experiences and what I have put into practice over the years – which I am going to share with you – that I can go into any business within any industry and make it a success. I always RISE ABOVE ALL because I choose and expect to live in abundance in every aspect of my life.

CHAPTER 1

Blank Canvas

What if I gave you a blank canvas and said, "Here. Do what you want with it." You would probably look at me like I had two heads. What would you do with it? You could possibly choose from the following three options:

Option 1) Leave it blank

Option 2) Let someone else take over and paint it

Option 3) Paint it yourself and add all the colors you wish and create whatever you want

Life is so precious when you stop and think about it and it really does compare to a blank canvas. These three options are always available to us, no matter the opportunity at hand; too often we let those opportunities escape us because the blank canvas in front of us is unknown and we feel intimidated and overwhelmed because we have no idea what to do with it.

A few years ago, I was introduced to intuitive painting by my beautiful, talented sister-in-law, Pam. Pam discovered intuitive painting after she and her family experienced the devastating news that her one-year-old daughter was diagnosed with leukemia. Their lives were turned upside down overnight, questioning God as to why this was happening to them and praying for a miracle.

After one full year of special care in a children's hospital, the then beautiful baby bounced right back and has now grown to be an amazing young woman. Pam put all her energy into this beautiful child but lost herself in the process. What she didn't know at the time is that her life was going to change drastically from that moment on. In her process of healing and finding her way back to reality, she started soul searching and began painting. Instead of being upset with God and the situation, she chose to accept it for what it was and just trusted that there was something for her to learn from the entire experience. It was then that she started healing by simply taking a blank canvas and letting her feelings and emotions come out. Today Pam is recognized throughout the world with her intuitive paintings and healing. If you'd like to learn more about her, visit www.rainbowrea.com.

Of course, when she first started this process, everyone thought she was a bit crazy, but as I watched her develop into this beautiful, giving and full of love human being, I became intrigued and had to see for myself what it was all about. I joined her for a meditation class one evening and I was invited to add some paint to one of her pieces of art. The minute my paintbrush touched the canvas, my heart discovered a new love. It was such a simple mark I had made on that canvas, but that's all it took for me to get hooked. I immediately came home, turned my basement into an art studio and started pouring my feelings and emotions out on blank canvas. Everything I looked at from that moment on was just beautiful. I would go for a drive in my car and the sky, the trees, the people, houses, birds showed their beauty to me and I was in awe of what I had discovered. I had just discovered OPTION 3; I discovered that I was indeed in charge of my life and I could paint it whichever color I wanted to.

For so many years, I had deprived myself of any hobby because I had convinced myself that my real estate business and my clients needed me and I owed it to them to be available 24 hours/day. I didn't feel I had any talent and I had no desire to search for any sort of hobby until that one evening at Pam's house. As soon as I got home at the end of each day, I would go to my studio and paint. Always starting with a blank canvas, I had no idea what the result would be, but I painted anyway. Sometimes, I cried; other times, I laughed. Some of my paintings looked like something a three-year-old would paint and others gave me a feel-good feeling. Some were meaningful and others meaningless.

The entire process was messy as I held nothing back and I would splatter paint everywhere. I had nothing to prove to anyone because I was simply painting for myself.

As I started sharing my paintings with family and friends, I discovered that my paintings were speaking to people and suddenly, my paintings were selling. I came to the realization that my blank canvas was a representation of my life: sometimes, old habits and patterns. Sometimes, I was painting in the moment feelings and other times, it looked like I was painting my future. There was no technique required: just my emotions and my intuition. Sometimes, I'd get upset because my painting didn't turn out as I wanted it to or I wasn't happy with certain strokes and they just didn't seem to fit with the rest. What it taught me was that each stroke occurred for a reason and there was no reason for me to fight the outcome because there were no mistakes in what I was creating, just as there are no mistakes in life. Everything that happens is meant to happen.

We have a choice every day to start with a blank canvas and create whatever kind of day we want. We can paint our day, our week, our month and our year with vibrant colors if we so choose.

Let's go back to my three options from earlier in this chapter.

OPTION 1: You can choose to leave it blank. Do you find yourself walking away from opportunities to then kick yourself in the butt and say, "I should have" or "what if"? Maybe you're afraid that making a drastic change in your life will create problems in other areas of your life, like your marriage, your job, your health or your finances.

The terror barrier kicks in and convinces you that you are not worthy of the beautiful colors that could be in your life. We were always told to stop daydreaming in school and to pay attention to the teacher. We were ridiculed and bullied if we showed any kind of beautiful colors because others were jealous that our colors were brighter than theirs. And we continue to sabotage ourselves as adults by allowing those fears or judgment and ridicule to run our lives. And what happens next? You decide to leave the canvas blank and continue to live your life with what feels comfortable to avoid stirring the pot anywhere else but then live to regret your decision years later when, in fact, there were no mistake or regrets to be had.

It's possible that you weren't ready. Maybe you had more to learn before moving on to the next stage of your life. Don't beat yourself up over what happened in the past and not painting that canvas when you had the chance because the beautiful thing about this world we live in is that we can start with a blank canvas any day.

When I made the switch from real estate to trucking, I remember sitting at my desk and feeling upset with myself for not making the decision sooner. I felt as if I had missed out on so much over the years. Even though I always had a hand in the trucking while I was in real estate, I was never there enough to give it 100%. I felt that if I had been there sooner, the trucking business could have grown so much faster, but then I realized that I wasn't able to do it any earlier. I wasn't ready. There were things I needed to experience in a different environment and I had to grow on a personal level before making that move. Learning to understand contracts and the art of negotiation. The skill of working with people and offering the service they deserved was what I needed to learn before I could take that next step. It was my gestation period.

We all go through a gestation period when we tackle something. There is no point getting upset with yourself because you feel that you started late in life; however, with the new skills you are learning, you can now approach life by listening to your intuition. You can now understand that you don't need to know it all before making the leap. You can just go with it. Put some color on that canvas, splatter all you want and you'll soon realize that you will figure it out as you go. The mistakes you are creating in your mind are not mistakes at all. It's called the journey to growth.

OPTION 2: You could let someone else take over and paint it. Has that ever happened to you? Rather than jump at the opportunity, you let it slip by to later find out someone else took that opportunity. Sometimes, it's someone you know. And that really hurts, doesn't it? It wasn't because you didn't want to take the chance. You simply convinced yourself that you didn't know how to paint that canvas when, actually, it didn't require any special skills. Or you had the skills at the time, but you didn't give yourself the chance to discover you already had it in you. How would you know? You didn't give it a chance.

I came very close to making a similar decision. Rather than realize I had the skills to run the trucking business myself, I considered hiring someone to do the job. I thought I was going to be a Realtor forever because that's what I knew. That's what was comfortable or so I thought. I didn't think I could replace the money I was making when, in fact, the money I was making as a Realtor never stayed in my bank account because I was always re-investing it in marketing myself.

At the end of the day, I didn't have that much to give up, but I convinced myself for years that the money would never be as good as what I currently had or I would never have the flexibility to do what I wanted. The idea of having to learn something new weighed heavy on me when, actually, learning something new became invigorating and exciting. It brought new joys, and mystery and I wanted to learn even more. I didn't realize I was in a prison. A prison I had created for myself. I didn't allow myself to have hobbies or to learn new skills; I believed that being an expert in my field was what I was supposed to be. WRONG! You can be an expert in many fields; you can learn new things and by doing so, you add more value to your worth. You can create this beautiful abstract painting with any color you want if you give yourself permission. Take the chance. What could go wrong? So long as you're not breaking the law, you will never end up in jail for trying something new. Suddenly, that painting you created is the biggest seller around and everyone wants one because what you created is irreplaceable. Become irreplaceable!

OPTION 3: You can paint it yourself and create whatever you want: My hope is that once you finish this book, you choose option #3. Instead of "I wish I had," you will say, "I'm glad I did'. Once you tap into your higher self of awareness, you will realize that life is all about taking risks. You will open yourself to so many opportunities you never thought possible.

Suddenly, you are living the life you were dreaming about in school when the teacher kept telling you to pay attention. The life full of bright colors, which everyone around you envies only because they are still stuck in the first phase of not touching that blank canvas. It's easy to become jealous or envious of others, but it's also not worth it. I decided a long time ago to stop looking at my competition and I will share that with you as we go along.

Concentrate on yourself, invest in yourself, learn new skills, learn and learn some more. Become indispensable, dream and dream big and keep focused on that beautiful piece of art you are creating. Don't be afraid to make mistakes along the way; there are no mistakes. That paintbrush wants to go where it wants to go. Your subconscious mind is leading it. Learn to let your intuition guide you through it all. And even if you make what you call a mistake, so be it. That's the only way you will learn. If you have kids, this should be easy to understand. You can't prevent a child from falling when they take their first step. They simply get back up and try again. Be that child; fall and get up again. The difference between successful people and not so successful people is that the successful ones dream and visualize their painting and then they make it come alive. They stay focused on those colors that make their day brighter.

No matter the option you choose, 1, 2 or 3, you will always experience sadness and laughter, feel-good feelings and sometimes, ugliness. Meaningful and some meaningless experiences, judgment and ridicule. Your life will be messy at times and other times, all will go as smooth as can be. These experiences will show up no matter what, so why not choose option #3 and just make the biggest mess you can make? Fill that canvas with the future you really want.

Remember, you can start with a new canvas every day. You're the artist! What will you create?

Chapter 2

When Pigs Fly!

I don't need to ask if you take the time to write down your goals. My guess is that you don't. In fact, 97% of the population doesn't know how to write goals. Today is your first day toward achieving your goals by writing them down. All sorts of studies have been conducted which prove that people who write down their goals have an 80% chance of achieving them vs just thinking about them. This number will vary depending on which study you read, but I choose to think big, so I'm going with 80%.

But what are goals? Really? Do you think that buying a house is a goal? It can be! But let me ask you this – do you own a house now? What kind of house do you live in and what kind of house do you want to buy? If your answer is that you live in a $250,000 home and you want to buy another one in the same price range but in a different neighborhood, I call that an ATTAINED goal. Why? Because you already know how to achieve that goal; you already have it. I would say your focus is to live in a new neighborhood rather than buying a house.

Now, if you tell me that you wish to have a $350,000 home, I'd say you're starting to get somewhere, but I still don't believe you are pushing yourself far enough and I call that the MEDIOCRE goal. If you can come up with financing for a $250,000 home, which you already own, the difference it would cost you per month to reach the $350,000 is minimal. Now, I know you're probably shaking your head at what I'm saying, but I'm right.

Think about it. You're probably looking at $1000/month in payments for your first house and now your 2nd house would be around $1400/month. A difference of $400/month. Can that happen easily? Yes, it can happen with a little extra effort on your part. You can either get a second job, sell more products or increase the rates on the services you offer. You could also go to the movies once a week rather than twice a week or reduce any other debt you currently have. A little bit of creativity will get you into that $350,000 house in no time. It is a goal, a believable one, but the goal I want to get out of you is meant to stretch you, to get you out of your comfort zone. You want to come up with a goal that's so big, you think to yourself, "when pigs fly"!!!!!!!!!! That's the goal I want you to come up with. Thinking that a pig could or would ever fly is CONTRADICTORY to anything we believe in. I want you to come up with a goal so big that it contradicts everything you've ever allowed yourself to believe in.

I know you're saying, yeah right!!!! That's stupid. Why would I want to do that? Why not? What's wrong with dreaming? What's wrong with visualizing yourself in a million-dollar home? It won't hurt anyone for you to think and dream it. In fact, it's probably going to fire you up so much that you will start attracting all sorts of opportunities your way. We are so brainwashed to think that we should only allow ourselves benefits according to our current status or our current environment that we turn our heads the opposite way when we are told to think big. We choose to leave the canvas blank or let someone else paint it. You say, my dream will never happen. I say, but what if it does????????

Remember I said we are meant to live in abundance? That could mean many things. I'm not only referring to money or a house when I talk about goals or abundance. It could be love you're looking for; it could be your body weight or a new job. We are not put on this earth to suffer. We are meant to enjoy life and experience its beauty. Have you ever come across someone who said they attracted their spouse into their lives by writing down in detail the qualities they were looking for in a partner? They sat down and probably wrote, *I want a handsome man, with blue eyes, blonde hair. Doesn't smoke and doesn't swear. He is honest and faithful. Loves me for who I am* and so on… and then in no time, someone shows up out of nowhere and the rest is history. I know many people who have done that – in fact, I'm one of them.

We are always looking for increase in everything we do, have and want. We want more hugs, more joy and laughter, more clothes, more cars. More freedom, more friends, more, and more and more. You can deny it all you want, but it's a fact. Don't shame yourself for wanting more. Give it all you've got and go for it!

I look back at so many people I considered friends over the years that have sort of slipped away from my life because either I outgrew them or we just didn't think the same way. I think a certain sense of maturity comes with our journey to growth and helps us realize who we want as friends going forward. I know I've concluded that I only want to surround myself with people who want better and more for themselves rather than make me feel guilty for desiring more of something or anything, for that matter. I'll never forget a comment from years ago as if it were yesterday when I was sharing my thoughts about something I wanted for myself and the feedback I got in return was "want, want, want" as if it was a bad thing. It struck me as so funny at the time that I believe it helped me grow even more. And I've come across many other comments over the years like "you're just spoiled" or "can't you be happy with what you have?" or even better "you're so high maintenance". These comments fall into the same category of bullying even when they are said by adults.

I can say that wanting something makes me get out of bed every day. It makes me look forward to what is coming, the unknown. It's exciting that I can make things happen for myself and I want to know how far I can take it. It's human nature to want and desire more food, more body strength, a good spouse and better results in just about everything we do in life. I say screw it. Be high maintenance! Being high maintenance doesn't mean you're a diva or high class unless you attach that stigma to it. My gosh, we are here to live, to love and have fun. Start now before it's too late. Paint that blank canvas already. The saying, "you are what you eat" goes hand in hand with "you are who you hang around with". Distance yourself from those who bully you from your journey into growth.

Let's think about "the flying pig" for a minute or two. Let's just say that for the next couple of minutes, I give you the freedom to dream. This is you and I; no one else is here. I'm asking you to think about whatever comes to mind when I say to you, "there are no restrictions to what you can have. All the money in the world is at your disposal. No one or nothing stands in your way; you can be whatever you want. I have a magic wand and I can make anything you desire appear." What does that look like to you? Describe it to me. Pretend you and I are sitting together over coffee and you are telling me in detail what your life looks like.

Your dream house, what color is it? What size is it? Single level or two-story? Does it have a pool?

Do you have lots of land? Any animals? What are they?

What does your dream job look like? How much money are you earning?

What do you see yourself doing for a living? Are you working for someone else or for yourself?

Are you selling something? What is it?

Your family, what are they doing in this fictional life of no restrictions? Do you have kids? How many?

Are you happy? Do you and your spouse laugh a lot?

Your friends, who are they?

Your hobbies, what are they?

Your body weight, how much do you weigh in this pretend world of flying pigs?

The car you drive, what color is it? What brand? Nissan? Honda? Mercedes? Ferrari?

Be specific as if you already have it all and customize it to what you want. My list of questions is just there to help guide you, but you may come up with more. Bring yourself to that magical world that you've been dreaming of since you were a kid. Put yourself behind the wheel of that car you've always wanted. Pretend you're revving the motor and going down the highway. Is it a convertible or a big motorhome? You're not hurting anyone by doing this exercise. No one even needs to know.

Now that you have it in your head, let's write it down as if it's already here. Like my mentor Bob Proctor says, you should always start with "I am so happy and grateful now that" and then start writing what it is you want. When you start with those words, you force yourself to write in the present tense; therefore, it feels like it's already yours. Sit down, grab a pen and paper or your laptop and get to it. Like I said, no one is getting hurt with this exercise. You're not going to end up in jail. You are just putting bright colors on that blank canvas of yours. Splash those colors. Make it juicy. Then carry that piece of paper with you in your wallet or your purse and read it every day.

Another mentor and friend, Peggy McColl, *New York Times* bestselling author, says if you want to go one step further with this, record yourself reading your desires. She calls it "Power Life Script". Record it and listen to it often, every chance you have. Today's technology gives us so many options to do that. Record it on your phone and listen to it on your Bluetooth in your car or while you're out for a walk or cleaning the house. Listen repeatedly until it becomes fixed into your brain. You will soon start believing it and wonderful things will start happening.

Be very careful, however, not to get caught up in the "HOW" this would ever happen. It doesn't matter. Remember we are just dreaming right now. You are just creating a new way of looking at life. Just as I was in awe when I started painting and everything I looked at was absolutely beautiful to me, you will start looking at things in the same way. So, even if you don't achieve everything you wrote down or recorded, you didn't fail. Everything has a gestation period and things come to us when they're meant to come to us.

You will soon find yourself being a different person, thinking and doing in different ways. You will start attracting new people and new opportunities into your life. Your awareness level and your intuition will finally be awakened and you will find yourself painting that canvas rather than leaving it blank. You will distance yourself from people who judge you and you will attract likeminded people into your circle. This will happen all on its own; the only effort required on your part is to listen to your life script recording every day.

By doing this exercise, you will realize that these dreams are no longer dreams. They're your new reality and once you begin experiencing this, you will want to share it with others. You will want the whole world to know this secret. That's when you truly start to shine. Just as I would see beauty in trees, birds, animals and the sky, you now see the beauty in people, you recognize their potential and you want to bring it out in them.

It's easy to recognize those around us who have no defined goals by listening to how they speak. They never see the opportunity in front of them. You will often hear things like:

"I can't afford that right now" or

"I would never be able to do that".

"All I want is to live a comfortable life".

"We can't have everything" or even better

"I'm too old for that now".

Whenever I hear these words, I feel sad. I come across so many people who think that their way of life today is what they must settle for, for the rest of their lives. So many would love to do something different with their lives, but they just can't bring themselves to take action because they think they need to know everything and do everything on their own. They get overwhelmed and nothing ever changes. Business owners go bankrupt because they never had a clearly defined goal. They are so caught up with what they lack, they forget they are sitting on acres of diamonds as Earl Nightingale says in his book *Lead the Field*.

I am fascinated by the concept of writing goals; I've been doing it myself for years. How else do you think I became one of the top 100 Realtors in North America as well as the recipient of the "Women Who Inspire in Trucking Award", an "Employer of Choice" designation now for two years straight? And, most recently, my trucking company is now recognized in "Growth 500 ranking of Canada's Fastest-Growing Companies". It wasn't by accident. I wrote my goals down and still do to this day and I make it happen.

I come across so many individuals who are afraid to think big because of their spouses. I was recently at a Bob Proctor seminar in Los Angeles and one woman was telling me how her husband was always bringing her down. It didn't matter what she wanted, he would find fault in it or convince her that she did not need it or deserve it. Can you relate to this? I need to make something very clear to you. What you desire for yourself is entirely up to you and no one else. You don't even need to share it with anyone. If you are avoiding dreaming or visualizing better for yourself because of what someone else is thinking, you are simply hurting yourself. If you're afraid to lose your spouse in the process, you've probably already lost him/her to begin with. Either way, your path is already planned for you. You either choose to make it harder for yourself or chose to embrace the opportunities life is giving you whether you like it or not. Your spouse has a journey of his own just as you do. I learned this the hard way when I was almost ready to give up on my marriage until I was able to make peace with the fact that I had to concentrate on myself and no one else.

I'm sure you've heard that "everyone who crosses your path was meant to cross your path for a reason". Sometimes, it's because we need to learn something from the other person or maybe, you were meant to help or teach them something relevant. Either way, your destiny is waiting. If your spouse is meant to be in your new reality, he or she will follow and everything will fall into place. If he or she is not destined to follow you to your next level and you try to fight it, it's going to make the journey harder for you, but believe me, whatever is meant to happen will happen at some point or another.

I'm fortunate that my husband is very goal oriented himself. I've never met a human being who is so determined to make everything positive around him. When I met him almost 20 years ago, he would often say to me, "why do you worry about money? They print it every day!" Isn't that a beautiful way to look at life? It's the truth. Money is printed every day. Another quote I came across lately is "Stop saying marriage is just a piece of paper. So is money, but you still get up every day and work hard for it".

My husband worries like the rest of us, but he overcomes it. Hardly anything scares him; he is probably one of the most goal-oriented people I have ever met. Why? Because he sees himself as a success. He doesn't let anyone paint his blank canvas for him. He sees the opportunity, he takes action right away and figures out how to make it happen along the way. This concept scares many people and I must admit that his level of goal achieving mind-set is sometimes overwhelming even for me at times, but for the last 19 years, we (as a couple) have never failed at anything. We had many setbacks, many obstacles, but nothing was ever looked at as a failure. In fact, the word 'fail" doesn't exist in our vocabulary. We simply don't allow it. We have fears like everyone else, we have problems, and struggles, but we get over the hurdle as fast as it came to us.

Do yourself a favor and never allow yourself to fail going forward. Remove it from your vocabulary. Live for yourself and no one else. Dream big!

Let me help you with this one more time:

I am so happy and grateful now that... (write in the present tense as if you already have it; it's already yours).

CHAPTER 3

No Room for Mediocre

I think you will agree when I say, it makes no difference which part of the world you live, what industry you work in or how much money you earn – Each one of us is experiencing economic changes to some degree or another and these are coming at us at high speed. Look at the tools we use to communicate and travel, for example, smart phones, electric cars and Uber. Even the way we handle money, email transfers, wire transfers, credit cards, debit cards, online banking and so on, are all part of the new age and the new way of doing business.

Change has always existed, but the speed it's now going makes it inevitable, yet it remains challenging for many individuals. We tend to look at things and say, "don't fix what's not broken". Why? Because change causes such an uncomfortable feeling that the average person tends to have a rebellious response toward it, almost to the degree of severe disruption at work and at play. It doesn't have to be this way. You can choose to ignore what's happening, but it could cost you a job, or you could embrace change and adapt to it with open arms.

Ignorance toward life in general, the world, cultures and even generations can be costly. It's not difficult to notice that many jobs have been lost due to automation. Starting today, I recommend you work on your awareness level toward life in general. Remember all those times you were driving in your car, and suddenly you realized that the entire drive was just a blur and you didn't even remember how you made it to your destination? Let's not go through life the same way. Instead, let's go through life purposely. It does take some effort, but it's no different than when you really wanted something badly like your first car or your first house. You purposely saved money to get what you desired. Now approach your entire life in the same manner.

When it comes to the business world, culture and generation play a big role in the development and success of a company. Let's put our attention on the different generations that form our typical workplace as an example. Have you ever noticed a vast difference in the age groups? Depending on the size of the company you work for, your workplace may consist of young adults fresh out of high school as young as 18 years old and the executives who could be in their 70s, enjoying work so much that they can't bring themselves to retire. Below are the five generations that are still working today.

The Traditionalists: Born before 1945. The traditionalists faced the Great Depression and WWII. They respect authority, they are disciplined and focused on family. They are used to doing more with less and were brought up to sacrifice their needs. Structure is what they know especially hierarchical structure. They were, and still are for the most part, the leaders and executives of many big companies today.

The Baby Boomers: Born between 1946 and 1964. This generation lives to work. They have strong work ethics. Very ambitious and they expect everyone else to be the same. They are rewarded by money and don't require much guidance. Saving for retirement was and still is of the utmost importance. Today this generation is known to be the wealthiest of all generations. Many of them are still business owners.

Generation X: Born between 1965 and 1976. Following in the footsteps of their baby boomer parents. This is the generation of duel income families but also of more divorces. They are in between investing for their retirement and living in the moment. Very hard working but more concerned about work and family balance. They like feedback and recognition but are less respectful toward authority. They are known as the "in between generation," as their birth years encompass a very short period. They started leading the way for the younger generation to come. They are still quite active in the workplace today and are intrigued by the younger generation's way of thinking and doing but still very concerned for their own retirement.

Millennials or Generation Y: Born between 1977 and 1995: They grew up as children of divorce. Parents tried to shelter and protect them. Entitlement is where they come from. They are highly educated, but they earn their money to spend in the moment. Less concerned for their retirement. Job sharing and flexible schedules were pretty much invented by this generation. They value their lifestyle and tend to be more risk takers. They would prefer to make the rules as they go. Very present in the workplace.

Generation Z: Born between 1996 and later: This younger generation is looking for the cool product, the newest on the market. They are tech-savvy, practically born with a smart phone in their hands. They are more open to racial, sexual and generational diversity. Cursive writing is not taught in school. They depend on technology for practically everything. They are the game changers for what is to come. This generation is leading the way and will soon be the new founders, executives and employers of this modern world.

Mix them all up and you have just created the image of your typical workforce. Each category shares some similar qualities that have carried over from generation to generation, but on the other hand, they also bring very different perspectives to the day-to-day operations of a business.

Understanding people and how they think and function is a difficult task, let alone five generations raised extremely differently. Some communicate in writing, while others never learned cursive writing, so they communicate by typing shorthand and emojis. Pensions and job security are extremely important to some; others live for the moment and don't worry about the future. Some raised families of 12 children and some have no interest in raising kids. It is imperative that we bring awareness to the diversity in the world around us and in our workplace. If we think creatively and tap into each generation's strength to move forward, everyone would benefit greatly, but many fail to do so. I've made bad decisions on behalf of my business in the past because I failed to recognize these differences. I remember dismissing a young man after two weeks of employment because he was always on his phone. I was getting complaints from other staff members that he didn't seem to be interested in anything. What we failed to recognize was that he was using his smart phone to take notes because that's how he was taught in school, while the rest of the staff at the time were still using cursive writing on notepads.

Here's another example. Years ago, only the executives made decisions on behalf of a company and it was mostly done behind closed doors. Employees were not encouraged to voice their opinion. Today, we are on a completely different path. Everything is expected to be transparent; employees are encouraged to participate and executives are expected to listen.

Awareness will make or break a business. It will make or break you as well if you don't work harder at noticing and adapting to changes. Just because we depend more and more on technology doesn't mean it has to control our lives, our lifestyles or a company's culture. In fact, we could learn to use it to our benefit and think creatively just like others have done and continue to implement all sorts of changes every day in order to stand out and beat mediocrity.

Let's study grocery stores for a minute. They now offer self-check outs for those who prefer quicker service and want to avoid lineups. You can also order your groceries online and just pick them up or have them delivered. Then we have online shopping. Everyone has heard the name Amazon, right? Genius idea! They make shopping extra easy from the comfort of your home and in some instances, your order is delivered the next day. If you don't need something that exact day, you may choose to stay home and wait for it to come to you. Right?

Financial institutes are now asking the public to use the ATM machines as much as possible rather than go to a live person at the counter. Just take a picture of your check and it's immediately deposited into your bank account via your phone. I recently ordered US money at my local bank for travel purposes and when I approached the counter, the attendant told me I could have ordered it online and have had it delivered directly to my door within a day or two. I remember the days when the banks closed at 4 pm. Today banks have introduced evening and weekend hours, so they can accommodate the public. It's now all about convenience and ease. All these examples are just the new norm and the new reality.

So, why is it that some can't keep up and others are growing bigger and becoming the new giants? Well, as I said, some accepted mediocrity and expected the world to remain the same forever. Others, like my examples above, have realized that there are new ways of doing business. They have studied their market and their competition and little by little, they started offering new services or products that make everyday life so much easier for everyone. Rarely will you see any business make drastic changes over night. Most changes happen with baby steps until they have accomplished their goal. Then a new goal is set, and they proceed further and that's how they do it. If they don't implement small changes on a regular basis, they will find themselves in what we would call a "pickle". Or if you look back at my blank canvas; those who choose not to make those small changes are really stuck in OPTION 2. They are letting others take over.

So, what's the BIG difference between the retail giant that just closed its doors versus a retail giant like Amazon that is booming? The retail giants who closed their doors remained MEDIOCRE in comparison to their competition! There was a huge lack of awareness. They may have experienced some excellent years, but they forgot to keep the momentum. They lowered their expectations and assumed everything would always stay the same forever.

You and I could face the same reality if we chose to be oblivious of the fact that we must embrace change; it's here and it's now. Not 10 or 20 years down the road: more like tomorrow and next week. There are new opportunities for you and I created each and every day, new jobs, new technology and new services. There are people who chose to think for a living; they don't worry about the changes as if they're a burden or a disruption. They instead embrace the new reality and work at making it even better than what it was before. What most people fail to understand is that we all have this thinking capability, but the average person is too scared to think.

Any business can create something just as big as Amazon or even Uber. You as an individual can do the same. Nothing is stopping you! Yes, change can be challenging, it can be costly, it can cause resistance, but only if you are lacking a sense of awareness and understanding. It's up to us, individually, to focus, to create, to study, to learn, to educate and to teach. Don't depend on others to think for you or wait for others to lead the way. Start your own trend, your own way.

People are not the only ones experiencing changes. All industries are being challenged. I'm talking about hospitals, refineries, manufacturers, school systems, transportation, automotive, the housing market and anything you can imagine. Highly unionized groups still exist today but are not as important to most people. Titles are now also less important; the average person wants to have a say or to make a difference, no matter their title, and they look for transparency from their leaders. Leaders who are open to this concept will survive this fast-changing world and those who refuse to accept could find themselves bankrupt and jobless. There is simply no room for "mediocre" anymore. NONE!

If you look up the definition of "mediocre," it says, "of only moderate quality: not very good." Is that what you want to be known as? I certainly don't! Ask yourself this question: If you were a business owner looking to hire someone, would you hire yourself? OUCH! That's a tough one for some of you, isn't it? It's not for me! I would hire myself in a heartbeat.

My definition of "mediocre" goes more like this: "of no extra effort, a lack of get up and go and a lack of understanding." Let's explore the "mediocre" person's affirmations vs the "leader's'" affirmations.

Mediocre employee affirmations

1) I don't care to make an extra effort at work. I'm not paid to do more.

2) Only the lucky ones stand out and end up with high paying jobs.

3) No one will notice if I call in sick, right?

4) No one cares about my opinion and ideas.

5) I'm just a number. My presence doesn't really matter.

6) I never understand the reason behind decisions that are made at work.

Leaders' affirmations

1) I know my hard work will eventually be recognized.

2) I love helping at work. I feel as though I make a difference.

3) I know that my office depends on me to show up at work every day. I must be there for my co-workers.

4) If I don't understand something, I ask for an explanation.

5) I love learning and studying.

6) I really feel as if I have a chance for advancement.

We need to put an IMMEDIATE STOP to "mediocre" attitudes or performances from ourselves and others. Even if your boss, manager, teacher or parent doesn't act like a leader, it doesn't mean you can't. The retail giants I speak about missed their mark when they failed to tap into people's strengths. They missed their growth opportunity by not recognizing that the world we live in today empowers others to be leaders rather than empowering them to be mediocre. They chose defeat because opening the doors to more leaders, more ideas and more creativity could mean chaos in their world if they are not equipped with the right attitude. Rather than creating new ways of doing business and having "when pigs fly" goals, they remained mediocre and chose to be completely inattentive to the fact that the world has evolved and the speed it is going at. It's not waiting for anyone or anything. This is critical for all of us to understand.

Work at being better today than you were yesterday. Learn something new each day. Put all the pieces together. Understand the importance your behavior and performance have on others. Learn to understand the process of your job and your industry. Put yourself in other people's shoes and learn to be empathetic. There is, however, one very important fact that I would like you to understand: "mediocre" and "human error" are two different things. Allow "human error," but do not accept or permit "mediocre". What we allow, we permit!

We should all embrace this modern world going forward and we should all step up our performances and our attitude a notch or two. Don't be afraid to RISE ABOVE!

Chapter 4

No Shortcuts – Law of Gestation

This is all so exciting, isn't it? You are now looking at the world in a whole different way. You want to get things moving. Don't you? And now I say to you, be patient!

All that's required is for you to keep your focus on your goal. Just keep visualizing it as though it's already yours. You don't need to figure things out on your own. The Universe does that for you. The more you believe and the more passionate you become, the more you attract and the faster things will start happening.

A puzzle takes time to put together, doesn't it? Some are easy and take an hour to finish and others are so complicated that they can take days and months to finish. The same applies to your goals. Everything you need will come together sooner or later. Piece by piece, the picture unveils.

Remember when you were a teenager and you looked at grownups and thought to yourself, "I can't wait to be that age", "I can't wait to be a grownup"? But you couldn't speed up the process. Life just isn't created that way. One birthday at a time, until eventually, you do make it to that grownup stage and you suddenly realize that it went faster than you thought.

Here's another example: We never eat from the garden on the same day we plant the seeds, correct? So, why do you expect your goals to come together overnight? Just because it's not happening right now doesn't mean it will never happen. In sales, they used to say, "a no today doesn't mean a no tomorrow". I lived by that quote for years and still do. I apply it to everything I work at. Today wasn't the day, but it could be tomorrow. It seems easy to accept when we think of the garden. For some reason, we can make peace with the idea that a garden has a gestation period, but when it comes to personal goals, we give up way too fast.

Don't compare your results to others either. They don't have the same goals as you. They are from a completely different DNA than you and what they have now or tomorrow changes nothing for you. Your goals may take longer, but it doesn't matter. Knowing that you worked so hard to accomplish everything you wanted will make it that much more enjoyable for you when you attain your goals. Everything comes to us when it's meant to come, not a minute sooner. Your willingness and determination to wait are what will make you or break you. How important is your goal?

Competition was a big thing in real estate. All monthly sales and listings would be posted on a board in the office for everyone to see. God help you if a new kid on the block beat your numbers for one month. That was devastating. I would often see Realtors just standing in front of this leaderboard day after day, analyzing each salesperson in that office. They were so infatuated by the idea that someone was doing better than them that their own results started declining at a rapid pace. The so-called "top performers" suddenly started losing their ranks and new Realtors started climbing to the top. They were so busy looking at what others were doing, they lost focus on themselves and they eventually lost sight of their own dreams.

This is very real! CAUTION! It's in every industry. You want to be competing with yourself not others. Luckily, I was able to notice this in the early stages of my real estate career and never really got caught up in it. I would simply not bother looking at the leaderboard. Not looking at it meant I didn't know what the others were doing. I was focused on myself and my customers. My results climbed throughout my career because I kept my eyes on my goals and it paid off.

Running a trucking business while looking at the competition could also play tricks on me if I let it. I often hear comments about what our competitor is transporting and questioning why that customer didn't give us the business. Then I turn it right around by saying, "did you ever stop and think that the competition is looking at us wondering how we got our business?" Rather than worrying about them, let's be the best at what we do and let them worry about us. Let's lead the way! Let them be distracted by us, not the other way around.

You should never want to take something away from someone or another business. That would be cheating the system. There are no short-cuts and if you think you must take something from someone in order to speed up your process of achieving your goal, you are doomed! Don't focus on stealing their customer; focus on finding new customers, creating new ways of doing business or doing something that no one else has ever thought of. If you operate from a place of creativity and growth, you will always find business and you will always achieve your goals. There is enough business, enough supply of any sorts and lots of inventions that have yet to be invented. Rise above the competition.

Are you able to distinguish reality from fiction? How often do you hear people tell you how busy they are? "OMG, I'm so busy. I don't have time for anything." But those people are never showing up on the leaderboards. What are they busy doing? Maybe they're busy making photocopies? Maybe busy taxiing people around showing houses to potential buyers who have yet to be approved for a mortgage? Busy browsing the internet for a quick fix? All I know is there seems to be a lot of busy people in this world and a lot of them are busy doing nothing.

It's so easy to get caught up in this. You start questioning why Ralph or Bob are busy and you're not! You distract yourself so much by trying to figure out what they are doing that you can't concentrate on your work. You just can't wrap your finger around it. Why are you slow and they're not??? It's driving you nuts. Guess what? Unless Ralph or Bob continue to show up on the leaderboard month after month, don't even bother asking them if they're busy the next time you see them. Don't even engage in that type of conversation. You're not doing yourself any favor. Bob and Ralph are busy for sure; they're busy distracting you. Stay away from them!

If by any chance, Bob and Ralph are leaders in the office, simply be happy for them! Say congratulations! You may want to ask them if you could take them out for lunch and learn from them. You want to ask them if they'd be willing to mentor you. You may even be willing to offer something to them, like your time for an open house in return for their time mentoring you. The more you invest time and effort in yourself, the quicker your goals will become a reality. Remember, you are no longer allowed to be "mediocre".

You are now a leader who makes things happen. Every day, every week, every month, you get up every morning and you just keep going.

Of course, there will be challenges along the way. This will devastate you and make you question everything you've worked for. But you need to remember something. A problem is only that, a problem! There is always a solution. Problems or obstacles usually come around to slow us down for a reason. I try and look at them as speed bumps. Maybe you were headed in the wrong direction and that speed bump appeared so you could change your direction. If you start looking at things this way, all your obstacles will be much easier to overcome.

Have you ever gone on a road trip where you suddenly had to make a stop for the bathroom only to find out that there was an accident just minutes ahead of you and if you had not stopped to use the washroom, you would have been involved in the collision? Could have been serious or maybe not. It doesn't matter. What matters is that you recognize that everything happens for a reason. And what is meant to come your way will happen when it's meant to happen.

We all had to start in kindergarten and then move on to grade 1 all the way to high school. Years ago, some of the smart kids were allowed to jump a grade and go faster than others, but that rarely happens today. Kindergarten and grade 1 to grade 12 is typically the gestation period for every child. To be ready to face the world, you have certain skills to learn. Like reading, writing, telling time, physics, math, science, arts and so on… You can't ask a child in grade 1 to go to work and expect him to be a surgeon. It just doesn't work that way and it's kind of silly when we think about doing that. So, when you find that your goals are taking too long, just bring yourself back to your years in school and remember why that process still exists to this day. We hardly ever hear of any kid skipping a grade now; they all must go through the same process and learn the same things. Only once that child has learned enough will he or she move on to learn how to earn money and live without their parents. Some will skip grades and some won't. That's okay. Be happy for those who move faster than others.

The unfortunate thing is that many skills are not taught in school. Personal growth, positivity, empathy, thinking, using your mind to its full capacity and goal setting are not usually part of the school curriculum. This tends to cause more delays in goal achieving because we are not 100% ready to face the real world right away. Unfortunately, as adults we are still faced with peer pressure, bullying, criticism and so on and that tends to throw us off our game. Bullying and peer pressure don't just happen in school; it follows us throughout our adult lives. The secret to achieving your goals is to RISE ABOVE all the bullying and criticism. It's up to you to find a way to embrace it as your journey to growth. The journey is your teacher! The journey teaches you those skills that were never taught in school.

If you are too caught up in the problem rather than in the lesson, you may miss your opportunity for growth. Learn to appreciate everything that happens. Yes, I'll say it! Learn the art of gratitude! Instead of asking why something is happening to you, ask yourself, "what do I need to learn from this experience?" There is always something to be grateful for and if you can't find a reason, make one up until it becomes second nature to look at life with gratitude. Be grateful for the journey, the lesson it taught you, the accident you missed, the person who smiled at you today. It's all part of the puzzle you are putting together. The trick is to be aware of each piece.

Schools provide structure to learn, but in adulthood, there are no more guidelines. We try to reach our goals and a little speed bump comes along and we're willing to give it all up. Why? Prove to yourself that there is a period of growth, that you will see the results no matter how long it takes. There are no shortcuts. Remember that.

CHAPTER 5

Self-Sabotage

A few months ago, I was exhausted, mentally and physically. I felt as though I had nothing left to give to my staff or my husband. The stress of running a business with my husband, working next to him 24 hours/day and the stress of dealing with a growing business and being responsible for 20-some employees was becoming overwhelming to me and I just couldn't find my way back.

I was blaming my husband, the economy, the world and anyone and anything around me. It didn't seem to matter how much studying I was doing on personal growth and business growth. I just couldn't seem to get a grip. There really wasn't anything wrong; everything was going smoothly. I wasn't sick, I wasn't hurt and the business was doing fine. We were still experiencing growth, but for some reason, I was going to work every day with a bad attitude and everything just seemed to irritate me.

I was looking for a break. I wanted some time to think, with no noise. I wanted to find a place where I could go for a week and stay in complete silence. I didn't know why. I just felt it was something I needed. I found a retreat called Vipassana Meditation, a 10 days of silence retreat. These are offered all over the world. I found one 12 hours away from my home and enrolled. No phones, no internet, no contact with the outside world, no books and no pens allowed. Just 12 hours/day of meditation and alone time. Some of my friends had bets that I would never last the 10 days, but my mind was made up. I wanted to be detached from the world for just a little while and recharge.

It was one of the most difficult experiences I ever put myself through. We typically don't go looking for these difficult experiences – they usually come to us – but I knew that stepping out of my comfort zone would bring growth: new knowledge and a new outlook on things. So, I embraced the challenge.

As I walked into my designated room for the next 10 days, I opened the door to find a room divided into six little cubicles. My bedroom was the size of 8' X 10', just enough space for a bed, night light and a bookshelf used as a dresser. The walls dividing each cubicle were only about ¾ of the way to the ceiling, so privacy was very minimal. My mattress was 1½" thick sitting on a board of plywood and wooden legs. We weren't allowed to make eye contact, no physical contact and absolutely no talking to anyone unless you needed to talk to the teacher or teacher's aids and that was kept to a strict minimum. I had no idea who my roommates were or why they were there let alone why I was there. I don't typically go to bed early at night, but for those 10 days, I would be getting up at 4 am every morning and going to bed at 9 pm.

Imagine sitting with your legs crossed for 12 hours a day while meditating. It was physically unbearable. Every bone in my body was aching. Thoughts from the past and the future were bombarding my mind and I had no idea what to do with any of it. Meals were all vegetarian, which was another challenge for me because I love to eat. Suppers consisted of apples, oranges and bananas only. Talk about getting out of your comfort zone. Two days into the retreat, I found myself questioning my decision-making skills. I wasn't sure I would be able to make it any further, but somehow, I kept going. Day five and beyond were even more difficult for me. I was bored to death, aching, happy and sad, but I continued forward. After all, I drove myself there. I went looking for this experience, so there was no reason for me to complain. Many gave up halfway through the retreat; some even gave up on day eight and nine. So close to the finish line, but sadly, they couldn't see themselves to the end.

Each day we had the opportunity to spend five minutes with our teacher to ask questions and the answer she gave me to the following question has made a huge difference on how I face life every day. My question to her was "what am I to do with all the thoughts that are crossing my mind, all the guilt and regrets that I have from my past and all the worries I have going forward?" Her answer was "your thoughts are just the radio playing in the background. When you're home working on something and you hear music playing in the background, it doesn't stop you from working, right? So, why are you letting your thoughts distract you?"

It's so true. We think millions of thoughts on a daily basis. We blame ourselves for things that happened a long time ago, we worry about the future and we make ourselves sick over things we cannot control. Why? There's nothing we can do about the past. Whatever happened has happened. That's it! It's come and gone. We worry about what the future has in store for us rather than having faith that all will work out as it always has. It's time to accept what was, accept what is in this moment and accept that the Universe has your back going forward. My outlook on my thoughts have changed since my conversation with this brilliant woman. I pay close attention to my thoughts. I just allow them to be there, tell myself it's the radio playing and I continue going forward. I know that whatever is happening will come and go. It's really that simple.

The Vipassana Meditation is a beautiful technique that teaches you to recognize the sensations in your body. You learn to observe each body part and the sensations that arise. What I learned along the way is that each experience we have in life is attached to a **feeling**. Each **feeling** creates a **sensation** that our body clings to. The mistake most of us make in life is we grab onto those sensations without realizing the negative impact they have on our body and brain.

We often talk about stress and it being a silent killer, but stress is not the only ailment. The minute we allow ourselves to accept a **sensation**, be it good or bad, we create a **craving**. The **craving** becomes a **negative or a positive sensation, which then turns into an addiction**. Our body wants more of that same sensation repeatedly. The body is not able to differentiate between a healthy or unhealthy sensation. It just wants more of it, which is **addiction**.

We tend to judge people who have addictions to drugs, alcohol, gambling and smoking, but we forget that there are so many more addictions in life. You can be addicted to food, to sadness, to love, to misery, hatred, lying, news and social media, technology and so on. Those are the addictions that are often missed because we can't see them. We can easily see someone drinking alcohol and recognize they're an alcoholic, but how often do you look at someone and say that person is addicted to hatred? Very rarely. We may suspect something isn't right, but we can't quite put our finger on the issue at hand.

And this is what we do, day in and day out. We experience an event of some sort and we are unable to control the sensation it creates in our body; therefore, it creates a knot. One knot over another knot until you have so many of them, you can't seem to function anymore. You can also call this the state of depression, DIS-EASE and unhappiness. You can't think straight, but your body doesn't know what's happening. It just knows that it wants more of the same thing you've been feeding it, be that a cigarette, drugs, hatred, fear, drama or misery. And because your body is so used to that same sensation, you continue to feed it, so it feels like it's surviving. You light up another cigarette thinking it will calm you down, but we all know it doesn't. In fact, the complete opposite occurs. You continue to show hatred toward others because your body is not recognizing love. Our job is to get rid of the sensations our body is addicted to, accept life as it is and realize that nothing lasts forever – just acknowledge the good and the bad and move on.

I was a smoker at a young age and just like an alcoholic is always an alcoholic, I'm a cigarette addict, but those 10 days taught me that I had many more addictions. I'm addicted to alcohol, gambling, food, fear, abandonment, negativity, drama, technology and much more. You're an addict as well. Your spouse is, your parents are, your neighbor, your boss. We all are. And the only way out is to recognize it and take action.

How many times have you promised yourself to go on a diet? It goes well for one to two weeks and suddenly, you give in and you eat a piece of that cherry cheesecake. Now you're feeling guilty. You're upset and disappointed with yourself and you attach guilt to that emotion. The guilt is your addiction more than the cherry cheesecake is. The vicious cycle starts all over again. Accept what happened. Next time, realize that the craving will come and go away as fast as it came and you'll soon realize you didn't even think about the cake. Don't waste your time on feeling guilty. You're just adding another knot. We all experience this self-sabotage at some point in our life. It can get out of hand fast if we don't recognize the sensations we are feeding our bodies.

Now that you are ready to paint your canvas with all the beautiful colors, you're working toward your goals every day and you're motivated.

You seriously need to be careful of the self-sabotage you create or allow to come into your subconscious. You need to stay on track and not let anything get in your way. Yes, you will have setbacks. I guarantee it! But now you're much smarter than you were before you started reading this book and you can overcome anything that interferes with your progress.

You will want to watch all the conversations you have with other people and yourself, for that matter. Make sure you surround yourself with like-minded people. Most of the world is stuck in these addictions. Surrounding yourself with the wrong people will delay your process.

Why were we not allowed to talk to others during these 10 days? Well, it's easy to figure out. It's human nature to want to share your experience with others. Once you start sharing, you compare and then your experience is easily altered because you find yourself wondering why your thoughts or sensations aren't the same as your friends. Another person could be feeling a tremendous amount of joy while you're experiencing major sadness. Your body could be aching and the other person's body is very relaxed. Then you find yourself completely confused, unable to just be in the moment and go through the process you first set out to accomplish.

The importance of being silent made so much sense when it was explained to me and I came to the realization that talking is really overrated. We talk to just talk. Most of our conversations in life are meaningless and of no benefit to anyone. We would rather cause drama or talk about others rather than deal with our own suffering or our own growth. If we do this every day, it becomes an addiction. Just like cigarettes or gambling, you are now addicted to drama or fear or resentment and you distract yourself with meaningless thoughts.

Decide today only to have meaningful conversations with others. Don't get caught up in self-sabotage. Yes, we are all guilty of this to one extent or another. For some people, it's a hobby and you want to stay clear of those people. The saying, "you are who you hang around with" is so true. You've come this far. Now you must be very aware of what sort of conversations you engage in.

Be conscious of your conversations with yourself as well. This is so important and crucial. If you judge yourself, add guilt to things you've done or continue to worry about things you can't control, you must – and I stress MUST – bring yourself right back to reality. Realize that unless you are bringing something of value to your conversation, it's not worth your energy or your time.

The world would be in such a better place if we approached every conversation with caution and really put a lot of thought into the words that we express to others and to ourselves. When you look at the world we live in, it's easy to see that society has become addicted to anger, betrayal, jealousy and hatred. We should want to engage in loving words and loving thoughts and only speak if it will benefit the other person or yourself.

We usually want to blame others for not accomplishing what we want. It's never our fault and we convince ourselves to no end that someone else is to blame. It must be the economy, the bad decisions from our world leaders or our spouse. WRONG again! It's absolutely our fault. It's 100% our fault. We are completely ignorant of the fact that we are the only ones who can control what we allow. If you choose to take your eyes off your goal, it's not because your friend told you to give up, it's not because of whomever the President of the United States is at the time and it's certainly not because the little demon in your head convinced you that you weren't good enough. You're the one who altered your way of thinking and you're the one who let yourself be influenced by someone else's addiction of self-sabotage.

My experience at the meditation retreat was difficult, but I learned so many valuable lessons . Now I know that when I find myself upset with the world or exhausted and mentally drained, it's usually because I took my eyes off my goals and forgot to look in the mirror to realize I created whatever is going on in that moment, in that day, that month or that year. It's a setback that can last a long time if you don't take charge right away.

I've concluded that I want to always be of benefit to myself and others. I want to come from a place of love and joy. Being alone in my little cubical with my thoughts was the best gift I could have given myself.

Remember that talking is overrated and you don't need to participate in anything that doesn't bring the best out in yourself or the world around you.

CHAPTER 6

Limitless Potential

If they could see me now! I'm referring to the people in my past whom I could have allowed to deter me from accomplishing great things in my life.

In my insurance job, I was told I would never be promoted because I was a woman and now look at me. I'm running a business that is recognized as a male dominant industry. I deal with million-dollar contracts, which are mostly controlled by countries I've never visited in my entire life. Top executives put their faith in me, my husband and my team. Gender makes no difference to them. They want and expect quality!

In real estate, I was recognized as having a very dominant personality to the point that some of my co-workers were scared to approach me. My clients loved me for my dominant personality. It meant I was looking after their best interest. I negotiated on their behalf to get them the best deal on the biggest purchase of their lives. But on the other hand, co-workers were intimidated. None of those Realtors and managers I had then understood how this affected me on a personal level. I felt misunderstood and alone because of it. I honestly thought I was being judged; deep down inside, I had so much to give and so much love to share with others, but I didn't think anyone wanted to acknowledge or see it. I could easily put the blame on everyone else, but in reality, I was the one who wouldn't allow them to see the person I'd come to appreciate today.

If only the teachers at school and university who watched me fall asleep at my desk could see that I really had potential to do great things. They probably thought there was no hope for me because I wasn't paying attention. Here's the thing; I had been paying attention to my parents who were running a business, to the environment and the entire world. Theory meant very little to me. I wanted hands-on experience. If they could see me now!

When I made the move from real estate to trucking, I felt challenged even more. Although my staff knew I was part owner of the company, they saw me as a Realtor, not as a leader in trucking. Any change I tried to enforce was quickly rejected because to them, I had no credibility in the trucking business. They weren't necessarily wrong. However, because I was not willing to give in, I was able to find a way to reach out to them. I was able to show that business is business and by showing them the real me, the person who has a big heart, who is truly concerned for their wellbeing, they eventually realized that I was on their side. The values and beliefs that I brought forward to them over time spoke for themselves. A male dominant industry can be very challenging for any woman. They used to see me as the boss's wife, but now I can say, they see me as a leader. I was able to gain their trust and bring them to the next level where the company needed to be and bring the best out of them, so they could grow and flourish in their own lives.

The team of drivers, office and garage staff I have now have truly allowed me to be my real self. I turned those perceived weaknesses of mine into strengths because of them. I am forever grateful to my staff.

Although I felt defeated on so many occasions, I was willing to walk alone. I was willing to stay true to who I really am. Many times, I could have given in and let others convince me to be who they wanted me to be. Luckily, I didn't give in.

None of this relates only to money and how much of it I can earn. It has to do with who I am as a person. For years, I was convinced that because I had a dominant personality, I was unable to feel emotions, love or give to others. Those beliefs were wrong! I was able to stop being afraid of what could go wrong and concentrate on what could go right. That's the secret to your infinite potential.

Fear of failure and of disappointment control our lives, so we stick with what feels good. We stay in our comfort zone, but it is our worst enemy.

We are on this planet for a reason. We are here to be creators. We are here to give of ourselves to others. To shine with every opportunity that comes our way. The more you face your fear; the more opportunities will come to you. If someone offers you a new outlook on life, take it. You never know what will come out of it. New people, new surroundings, new beginnings will appear to you. You will suddenly become more aware of how big this world is and how much it has to offer you.

There is so much more to life than just doing the same mundane thing, day after day. If you choose to stick with the same routine, you will continue to get the same result. Getting up in the morning, going to work all day, coming home, cooking supper, doing homework with the kids and going to sleep is a daily routine for all of us. If you don't add a little pizzazz to your routine, you will soon find out that life has passed by and you've gotten older and are just sitting at home waiting to die. I know it sounds depressing when I say this, but it's reality.

I refuse to live my life this way. I refuse to accept the notion that I'm working hard every day and my only reward at the end will be to wait to die. We all will come to that point in our life, but let's not get there sooner than we have to. It's never too late to have dreams and goals. You're never too old to paint that blank canvas and you never have to say, "I can't have it all". You can have anything you want if you are willing and able.

Continuous growth is what I'm looking for. You will often hear Bob Proctor say, "study". What he means is educate yourself, read, travel and explore.

Read books that will add value to your life. Study what they say. Bob Proctor studies books in a way I never would have thought. He analyzes each paragraph of a book carefully; sometimes, he'll read the same paragraph every day for 30, 60 and 90 days or even a year. He does this so he can fully grasp the meaning of what the writer is trying to say. This may not work if you're reading star or gossip magazines. I don't care how celebrities live their life, first because whatever is written about them is probably not true and second, they should be allowed privacy just like we have. Books that bring value are about personal growth and business growth.

Travel as much as you can. It's a big world we live in and there is so much beauty in it. If you're always waiting for the perfect time to travel or for when you have more money, you are robbing yourself of knowledge. You will never truly understand the impact the rest of the world has on your life if you don't travel. I love traveling and I haven't done half as much traveling as others do. Take it all in – the cultures, the education, the scenery. I always thought I had an advantage over others because I could speak French and English. At one point in my life, I was able to read music, which I believe to be a third language, but I stopped practicing. It would take a lot for me to read it again, but it's not impossible.

In my travels, I've come across people who were raised to speak a minimum of four to five languages. It's nothing for them, but my, oh my, the opportunities that are out there because of it. Other countries go to the extent of punishing their people because they can speak more than one language. They try to separate them from each other. Some world leaders embrace language because of the possibilities it creates and other leaders try and isolate its people because they are completely ignorant to the world around them and what it has to offer. Traveling has helped me to appreciate the differences around the world; language is only one example.

When we think of transportation, we think mostly of cars, trucks, motorcycles and buses, but it's so much more than that. We have planes, trains, ships, bicycles and so on. Think of all the food that's delivered to restaurants and grocery stores all over the world. Some can only receive these goods by boat, others by planes because of their isolated locations, while others are easily reachable by transport trucks. All of the products we buy are delivered via some sort of transportation and the logistics behind it is mind-blowing. I was only able to recognize and appreciate the process and the enormous task behind this through my travel experiences.

Give yourself the gift of exploration and education. I'm not talking about going back to school; I'm talking about the school of life. Understanding how we live compared to other parts of the world is astonishing and you will soon realize that there are so many opportunities out there. You can't expect to grow if you continue to confine yourself to your way of life as if it's the only way.

Once you start learning and growing, your job is to share that with others. Remember growing up and being told that you had to share your toys or your snack? Now, share your knowledge. Give of your time and energy to others. You will grow even more because you're helping someone else.

This planet we share has infinite possibilities. Everything around us is energy. Someone creative thought about the chair you are sitting on, the computer you work on, the smart phone you text with, the paper you write on, etc. Imagine all the potential ideas that have yet to be created. You may not be an inventor and that's fine. But you are a creator. Create the life you dream about. Create the love around you that everyone envies. We tend to take for granted everything we work with in the run of a day. Take electricity, for example. We can't see how it's made, but because of it, we are able to see through darkness. Do yourself a favor and pretend that you can see things that don't yet exist. Believe in things that are not there yet. Believe in your goals as if they are already a reality. Fake it until you make it. Bring yourself as far as you can and then you will see how much farther you can go.

Go about your day trusting that the Universe has your back. Know that each move you make and each step you take is for a reason that's already set in place for you. If you take the wrong turn going to work, understand that it was meant to happen. You were either meant to avoid an accident along the way or you were meant to witness something else on a different route. Awareness is what will bring you farther. When you're aware of the fact that the wrong turn happened for a reason, you will start to understand how life going forward should really be lived.

Our minds are our biggest tool, yet most of us are afraid to think. It has been said that only 1% of the population thinks, 3% of people think they think and 96% would rather die than think. We go through life underestimating our full potential. We are afraid of thinking and of being alone with our thoughts. We are afraid of how awesome we can be because we think we are not worthy. We are not exercising our mind enough. If you take the time to shift your thinking one thought at a time, you would be amazed at what you could accomplish. BE quiet and pay attention to your true self. Recognize that everything you need to make your dreams a reality is already inside you.

The quality of life you desire to live depends 100% on you. You can choose to think negatively, but you can also choose to think positively. It takes the same effort for either one. Never be satisfied or settle for anything. Life doesn't stand still and your efforts don't stop just because you become comfortable. There is more, lots more, and it's up to you to either open the door to possibilities or keep the doors shut.

I approach life with intensity and somewhat with obsession. I know that there are many things I'm unaware of around me. I do what others don't want to do. I refuse to quit and I control my destiny. I continue to work at a pace that gets me results and then my work just becomes a passion. I want to shake things up and bring forth something that's never been seen before.

Those things and thoughts you have imagined for yourself all these years can be real. See, our mind knows what it knows. There is no way I can think of something as long as it's unknown to me, so it's my job to explore the world around me so I can fill my mind's database with as much information as possible. Therefore, I create more ideas. The more ideas I act upon, the more opportunities I create as well.

If you are afraid to go after something because it requires work, you will always live a challenging life. Nothing comes free, but trust me, the work it requires becomes easier and much more fun when you know what you're aiming for. That big goal of yours is worth your time and efforts. We tend to give up too easily, when we should have just tried one more time. If you continue to think negatively, you will always find a reason why you can't go after your goals. You will never notice the doors that are opening or have already opened around you.

Did you ever hear the story about Thomas Edison? He was sent home from school one day with a letter addressed to his mother. His mother opened the letter and started reading it to her son. She read, "your son is a genius. The school is too small for him and there are not enough teachers to train him. Please teach him yourself". He grew up believing in himself and Thomas Edison became one of the world's biggest inventors, including the light bulb, motion picture cameras, phonograph and so much more. Years went by after his mother passed away and while browsing through some old boxes, he came upon a letter addressed to his mother. The letter read, "your son is addled (mentally ill). We will not allow him back to school." Because of his mother believing in him and turning the story into a positive one, she helped her son become a genius. Today we all benefit from his inventions.

Success and money, love and health, begin with our imagination. If you don't start seeing it for what it is, and if you restrict your growth to what you have access to today, you will never see an increase in your bank account or a better marriage or better health. Your imagination will take you far beyond what you know today if you just allow yourself the right to dream and believe in something that is not yet a reality.

What is success? According to Earl Nightingale: "Success is the progressive realization of a worthy goal or idea." Really study this quote. **Progressive** – take one step at a time. Take action toward something. **Realization** – becoming reality. **WORTHY** – something that is worth your time and efforts. **GOAL or IDEA** – those creative thoughts you have or the dreams you've been having. That's the definition of success. It's not how much money you have or how much more education you have compared to someone else. Success is what you make it.

The biggest challenge for each one of us is questioning how we would ever attain such crazy "when pigs fly" ideas. Don't think too far ahead; concentrate on the present. Maybe the 24 hours in front of you to start with. Make the most of every day. People often ask me, "how do you manage to do so much?" "Where do you find the time to do everything you're doing?" My answer is that I take advantage of every minute and every hour of every day. That simple. It doesn't mean that I'm always working; taking advantage of every minute of every day is also taking control of my thoughts when I'm by myself or making the best of the value I bring to others when I'm in their presence. Yes, I do take time to relax and rest. That's my recharge time for myself. If I'm at rest or in relax mode, it's because I've been working my little heart out so I can reward myself with a little break. You need to do something every day, every chance you have. Then and only then will you see the infinite potential in front of you. When you're tired, take a break, but never lose sight of your goals and when you're on a break, make sure you treat yourself right by thinking positive.

Your only limits are the ones you set for yourself. If you don't feel over-whelmed from time to time or if you don't feel like you're in over your head, then you are not growing. Growth and change is uncomfortable, but if you learn to embrace it, you will reap the rewards.

If it isn't broke – break it! Create a new way! There is no special power required, just curiosity.

PART TWO

CHAPTER 7

Take Action

If you can think it and feel it, you can have it! If a thought or a new idea crosses your mind, it can be real, no matter how silly or contradictory it may sound to you at the time.

So often, we attempt to start a project or reach a goal with no real vision of the final result and we get lost. Lost because there's no plan of action, no direction or your goals are simply not big enough.

You've heard the saying, "where there's a will, there's a way". We have reached a point now where it's time to act. I've allowed you to dream about those big goals of yours. Now you need to turn those dreams into form, into reality. If you really want it, able and willing, you will do everything you can to get it. If you're not in love with your goals, you will find excuses. Excuses are synonymous to procrastination. Why do we procrastinate? Because we can't put the whole picture together or we're lacking a clear and defined plan.

You, yes, you, you have everything inside you: infinite potential to accomplish whatever your heart desires, no matter your age, no matter your present situation, no matter what country you come from. None of that matters. A positive mind is all you need. It won't always be easy and it will demand a lot of work, but it can happen!

If you are reading this book, you're probably looking for a new direction in life. You're looking to rise above all the negativity around you and you've decided to be a success in all aspects of your life. If you're looking for change, you need to create change. Continue to do the same thing and you will continue getting the same old results. Change doesn't have to be drastic. It can be incremental. One step at a time, one new habit at a time.

You will need to discipline yourself and your mind. When your little demon or your family and friends are trying to convince you to give up, you need to be ready to stand alone and stay true to yourself and your goal. You need to push that demon away and not let it control you anymore.

Think of yourself as a magnet. Approach each day as if you attract good in everything you do and everyone you cross paths with. Like attracts like. If you continuously think of problems, you will attract more problems. Constantly think of illness and you will always be sick. Poverty and your bills will keep adding up to bigger debts. Once you understand this concept, the possibilities in front of you are limitless. If you turn it around to a positive outlook, good people come into your life, good opportunities and lots of money. And you will start receiving just what you envision. It's the universal Law of Attraction.

You will be tested from time to time and you will need to make some sacrifices. Life is not always fair. Sometimes the sacrifices are small and other times they are major. That's when you get to see how important your goals really are. If you are willing to put your favorite TV show aside for your goals or if you're willing to miss a special event because you need to work, you know you're headed in the right direction. Remember, it will often get very uncomfortable before you attain your desired result. But it will all be worth it in the end.

Old ways will not open new doors. If you continue to say, "I've always done it this way," you will never rise above. Successful people understand this process. They understand that success is just on the other side of fear. Fear is most often the little demon I've referred to. Fear doesn't want you to leave your comfort zone. Many people have a fear of heights, but occasionally, they will face that fear and take a chance. They climb the ladder or they go on the Ferris Wheel and then realize it wasn't as bad as they thought it would be.

I can guarantee you that I would not have accomplished half of what I've accomplished so far in my life if I had never faced fear head on. I now reap the rewards, but I also know that fear is always going to be present every time I want to accomplish something new. There are, however, some fears that I'm not willing to give into. For example, I'm terribly scared of snakes; you will probably never see me touching one either. That's a decision I'm willing to make. I also understand the consequences of my decision. At this point in my life, I don't see the point of touching a snake and I don't see how it would add more quality to my life. However, if for some odd reason, one day I decided to own a pet store, touching a snake may be a good idea. It would then benefit me to conquer that fear of snakes.

There is always a choice. It's up to you to decide which fears are worth conquering and which ones aren't. We all have them. I don't know what lies ahead for me or if there ever will be a need or reason for me to touch a darn snake. I certainly hope not, but then again, an opportunity may come to me one day where I may recognize that there may be a benefit to it and I will have to decide at that time.

Decisions are part of life, from what time we decide to get up in the morning to what we eat for lunch, what we say to our boss, which road we take to go home or if we'll go to the gym that evening. Decisions are imperative. The lack of decision making is still a decision. You chose not to decide. Do you see how this goes? You're in charge. So many people fail to recognize this.

Rather than blaming others or situations for your behaviors or misfortunes, take a good look in the mirror. The person you see in there is the only one who can make change happen. You're the only one responsible for your environment and you can only blame yourself for being poor, for being miserable, jobless or unhappy in your marriage. There is no lack of anything in this world. Only our thoughts create lack.

A mediocre person will most likely always pity themselves. Their words will be louder than their actions. But if you chose to be a leader, your actions will speak louder than your words. You don't have to share your dreams with everyone. You should instead choose to show them. If you do little things every day to get you closer to your goals, everything around you will start to change. People will notice and suddenly, they want the life you have. They will ask you what you did differently. They will want to know more and the next thing you know, you have a bunch of followers. Lead by example. If you continue to engage in poor conversations that don't bring any value to you or if you chose to surround yourself with people who bring the worst out in you, nothing will change. Choose to go in the opposite direction. It's not by doing one thing once that you'll notice a change; it's by being consistent.

Change happens over time. Set a clear foundation, a clear plan of action. You can't build a house with no foundation. At least not in North America. You usually have a plan to go by and you must follow that plan if you want a solid, well-built home.

The next few chapters are dedicated to the practical side of rising above. We've explored the conscious part of thinking in part 1. Now you need to find a way to put it into practice. Implementation of new ideas in your everyday life is what will get you closer to your goals.

It doesn't matter if you're a stay-at-home mom, a secretary, a manager, executive or business owner. You can be a leader in the eyes of your kids. A leader at the office among your peers and it can be in any industry.

If you tend to say, "I'll try", consider removing that word from your vocabulary altogether. There is no more trying; that's a mediocre approach. You either do it or you don't. You must want it more than you fear it. Don't wait for someone else to lead the way. Take charge.

The only thing I want you to do is continue to keep your eyes on the prize. Continue to visualize your new life. Don't get distracted by how you are going to accomplish it. That's not important. The Universe will take care of that for you. All you must do is show up with a positive mental attitude. The rest will come all on its own. Taking action means you are willing to do whatever it takes. It means you are ready to discipline yourself, to make sacrifices and implement new ideas and new ways of doing things. You are willing to change some old habits and create new ones. You are willing to face all adversity, no matter what. Others will try to throw you off your game – they will try to distract you – but you now know better. You finally have a solid foundation and well-defined goals.

Creativity comes in all forms and sizes. You can be a creative mom or a creative entrepreneur. The ideas I'll be sharing with you are meant to spark some sort of interest or challenge. You may want to use some of my ideas or you'll find a way to create your own. Take and make use of the ideas that resonate with you and leave what doesn't click behind. Trust the process and believe in yourself. You are much stronger, smarter and more creative than you ever thought possible.

CHAPTER 8

Consistent Momentum

Consistency is the key to your new future. When your goal becomes important enough, you will do everything you can to make it happen. To keep your momentum, you must be as honest as possible with yourself and recognize when it's time to reach out for help.

If you decide to quit along the way, you will find yourself right back where you were before. Where you were before is where you were looking ahead wishing you could be your new improved self. NO point going backwards – nothing is happening behind you. It's all in front of you!

You are not practicing consistency if you only work when you feel like it. There must be a conscious and consistent effort on your part. You're not looking for perfection in this case. What I think makes people procrastinate so much is that they expect perfection right from the start. Remember, you don't eat from the garden the same day you plant the seeds. Unless, you are lucky enough to win the lottery overnight, that's the only way you will see immediate results which can also bring really bad circumstances if you don't know how to deal with such results. Life is not about winning the lottery. It's about the journey to get you to where you want to be and enjoying the moment.

If you're ready to embrace this new challenge, I recommend you start looking for guidance. Hiring a mentor or a coach was the best thing I did to keep myself on track. I've had many mentors over the years as I've been practicing this for quite some time.

A mentor is a person who sees your potential and helps you recognize it. You want a mentor who's not afraid to tell you exactly as it is; otherwise, you are wasting your money. A great mentor is one who believes in you when you don't and he or she will stretch you to your full potential. Sometimes, you can find a mentor in a friend you have high respect for and other times you have to dig a bit deeper and farther to find the right one. As they say, if you want better results, hang around those who have already succeeded at the same ideas you visualize for yourself.

In my sales career, I was often introduced to motivational speakers and attended many seminars and conventions: some of the names you will recognize I'm sure. For example, Bob Proctor, whom I have mentioned many times throughout this book. Wayne Dyer, Stedman Graham (Oprah's boyfriend), John Maxwell, Jim Rohn and I've read many books from Tony Robbins, Zig Ziglar and so many more.

I'm the type of person who doesn't like to watch a movie more than once. However, when it comes to personal growth, once is simply not enough. Repetition is key. Why repetition? Because you can only hear what your mind is ready to hear at that present time. Your mind tends to wander as you listen to someone talk. We relate to the words and suddenly, we're daydreaming or as they say, we go to La La Land, but the speaker doesn't wait for you to come back to reality. He continues to talk and you're missing everything the speaker had been saying for the last 15 minutes. Remember when you were daydreaming in school and the teacher would call out your name and you had no idea what the question was? It's the same thing. You were distracted by something the speaker said or something you were reading. You missed every other little important detail and there's no rewind button in a live session. Repetition is imperative. I've heard Bob Proctor talk many times now. I've heard many of his stories and yet every time I'm in his presence, I hear something new. It's not because he never said it before. It's because I was somewhere else when he said it.

For years, my focus was money and how to get more of it. When I attended some of these speaking events, my mind was geared toward money and nothing else. I wasn't getting the full picture. The environment I was in at the time pretty much dictated what I was ready to learn.

Sales are highly competitive in nature. Most salespeople live on a commission-based salary and they go day after day trying to support their families for the week or try and outdo their co-workers at the end of each month. They want the awards that come along with the success. I know because I was one of them. In real estate and any sales for that matter, you're only as good as your last transaction. Once a transaction is done, you must work hard at finding another customer who will trust you enough to give you their business. Doesn't matter what you're selling. Your results are highly dependent on you showing up day after day, because people want to deal with you and no one else.

The mentors I was seeking back then were mainly focused on sales tactics and how to make good money. I learned not to be afraid of a phone. I made a lot of cold calls over the years and I learned how to door knock effectively. I had a script to follow and I can still remember the beginning of the script: "When do you plan on selling?" This question was definitely not a yes or no type of question. It required a reasonable answer. Salespeople often feel awkward following a script because it doesn't seem natural, but with repetition comes a sense of ease. Those who were willing to follow the script and use it consistently were usually the ones on the leaderboard each month. I would never be able to tell you how many doors I've knocked on or how many people I've called upon to ask if they were interested in selling their home. The same questions were asked each time and I would either create an immediate customer or a lead for the future. I was able to recognize that a "no" today doesn't mean a "no" tomorrow. Everyone goes through some sort of change in their lives; some get divorced and need to sell their house. Some have babies and need a bigger house. I may have knocked on their door or called on the wrong day, but things change, and if I understand this, I'm not worried about asking the same question to the same people three months down the road.

Having a mentor increased my self-esteem and self-confidence and enhanced my careers to a level that I'm not sure I would have done without the techniques they taught me. Many people just look at training or mentoring as an expense that they can't afford. I'm telling you right now; it's an expense you can't afford to decline or avoid. Spend $1000 toward extra training or mentoring and you will get back $10,000 in earnings. I would dare say I guarantee it, but really it comes down to you and if you're willing to do what's asked of you. Spend $10,000 and you'll probably see an increase in the 6-figure income. I've invested hundreds of thousands of dollars and it's resulted in millions of dollars over the years, but that wasn't by accident. I took it upon myself to put into practice what I was taught. Every time you expose yourself to more training and education, you learn something new. As you grow, your mind will make room for more knowledge and you'll be ready to hear a new version or a new way of looking at things.

In my last few years in real estate, I was mostly working by referrals and repeat clients. If a new client called me off a sign, and they were not originally referred to me or a past client, I would then pass the client onto a co-worker and I would help them grow their own real estate career. Although I was successful and had an established clientele, I was not the person I wanted to be. I was focused on the wrong thing – MONEY. I was always ethical and looked after my client's best interest, but on the other hand, on a personal level, I had become self-centered, selfish, greedy and, as mentioned before, very dominant. Today, I look back and realize that there was so much more I could have learned only if I had known better. But I only knew what I knew. I wasn't open to anything else. Money meant survival. It meant recognition, awards and material things. I wasn't ready to learn how to be a decent human being.

If you're obsessed with or if your love of money is more important than anything else, you will always be looking at your competition. You'll always be looking at taking something away from someone else. Most of the population operates in this manner because money means survival. We need money to pay our bills and to provide for our families. The efforts are geared in the wrong direction. Unfortunately, some people learn the hard way. And they only make a shift once it's been forced upon them – when they've hit rock bottom and there's no other place to go from there but up. These stories are meant for you to recognize that you should not wait until you've hit rock bottom to make a drastic change in your life. Take charge and recognize that help is here for us now. If you seek it, you will find it.

My days spent in sales depended solely on my efforts. I didn't work in a team environment. I worked by myself, in my car with the occasional client. Suddenly, I'm sitting at a desk, with employees looking to me for leadership. I wasn't prepared and wasn't equipped for the change. Something was missing. I realized that I had gone far too long without a mentor. I needed someone to lead me just like my employees needed me to lead them.

I searched for the names I remembered from all the conventions I attended and there he was on my computer screen: Bob Proctor. I am so grateful today for being able to recognize that I needed help. I didn't wait until I sank and failed. I took charge. I enrolled in many, and I mean many, trainings and I invested a lot of money in order to bring my business to a whole new level, but I also gained so much more than that. I found myself in the process. Of course, money is talked about quite often, but it's also now looked at as something that appears on its own once you understand how to keep the momentum of doing certain things in a certain way.

Do yourself a favor and read the book *The Science of Getting Rich* by Wallace D. Wattles. This book had a profound effect on the life I live today. I followed Bob Proctor's instructions to read certain chapters day after day until it became a reality in my own life. Getting rich is not about money and how much you can earn; it's about your mental state and the changes you can make along the way that will bring you to money and success.

Here is what I discovered as I read this book and how I perceived it to make an impact in my life.

1) **Always leave people with a sense of increase** – Give every person you meet a reason to want more. Give them a sense that you bring value to their life, be it on a personal level or a business level. It really all comes down to giving of yourself. We often connect giving with money, but it's not at all. Giving of yourself really means you are giving of your time, giving of your knowledge to help another person. You can, if you so choose, give in a monetary aspect, but you don't have to. Bring joy and respect to other people. Give them a deal. Give them a smile. Give them a reason to come back based on how you speak to them. Remember I said that you should only engage in loving words and bring value to the other person you speak with? Speak in a positive tone. Offer help and hope to someone in need. These are simple methods of giving someone a sense of increase.

2) **What you want for yourself you want for others** – I love seeing others succeed. I love seeing them grow. Jealousy toward others will never serve us. Don't keep all your knowledge to yourself. Share it and help someone else grow. Here's a secret. There will always be someone better than you. There will always be someone prettier than you or smarter than you, so get over it. It will only bother you if you let it. If you want to be a success, help others become a success. Only

by giving will you receive more. Stop this competition of outdoing another and start sharing and helping. I share everything I can from my studies with Bob Proctor with my staff. I'm rewarded every day by witnessing their growth as individuals because they know how to set goals and they want to accomplish great things in their lives. They now come to work with intent rather than just to work for money.

3) **Stop competing and start creating** – I touched on this a bit in a previous chapter. If you're competing, you are taking your eyes off your goals. There is enough business for everyone. There is enough food, enough space in the world for each one of us. Why is it that one business owner can do so well and another one in the same industry down the road is ready to shut its doors? Someone is doing something right and the other isn't. One business is being creative and finding its own way by offering discounts, newer products and services and the other business can't think of anything different.

How many service stations do you have in your city? There's probably one at every street corner. How do they all survive? The successful one knows that the economy is between his own two ears, so he creates his own customer base. They may offer more groceries, a free car wash with their purchase, lottery tickets, full serve at the gas pumps and so on while the service station on the other corner never upgraded their pumps to offer payment by credit card, maybe they don't offer public washrooms or they don't sell cigarettes. One is thinking creatively and understands that with a little bit of investment and creativity, he will bring new customers to the door. The other service station just can't see past what they currently offer and what they have always done. The owner worries too much about what it will cost to invest in something new, which results in a fear of a lack of money, so he continues to be distracted by others rather than focusing on what he can change. He's looking at his competitor as his enemy. He's concentrating on defeat rather than putting all his efforts into his own business.

4) **Gratitude** – This is not a new word. We often hear about gratitude, but unless you practice it daily, even when it's difficult to find something to be grateful for, you will always have a hard time.

A few years ago, my city was devastated by a young man who was quite troubled. He was seen going down a street with a rifle in his hand, dressed in camouflage. This young man shot and killed three of our male local police officers. They never stood a chance. He was ready and waiting for any officer of the law to come his way. He then went running and a manhunt was underway for about three days. Our city was shut down. Wives were suddenly widows and kids without fathers. The citizens were devastated and everyone went into hiding until this gunman was finally captured. Today, he serves a life sentence in prison for the killings he committed.

It's a sad story and many people's lives have been changed from that terrible event. I too was hurt even if I didn't know those men who were killed, but I did have many friends and clients who were police officers and it made me realize that our lives can change in an instant.

I was so grateful for the people in my life that were home safe and I wanted to make sure that going forward, I would always find a reason to be grateful for something or someone. I proceeded to set myself a reminder on my smart phone for each evening at 9:55 pm. Every night at 9:55, my phone sends me a reminder to be grateful for something. On my screen, I see "Today I am grateful for" and then I think about my day and I chose something that happened that I am grateful for and I proceed by finishing the sentence. I have been doing this for years. Now, being grateful for something or someone is part of my daily routine and it comes so naturally that I don't really need my phone to remind me, but I refuse to delete it. I want to make sure that I never go another day of my life not being grateful. Some days, I'm grateful for small things like a smile someone gave me and other days for really big things like having my family close to me, or for safe travels and for a roof over my head. I find myself on many occasions either sitting at my desk, driving in my car, lying in bed at night and having a huge sense of gratitude for the life that I live, for the people in it and for the beauty Mother Nature has blessed me with. I recommend you do this right now and set yourself a reminder on your phone to make this a daily routine.

The more I studied these chapters, the more they became part of my life. Suddenly, I was able to recognize the beauty, talents and knowledge in others. I came to realize that I was no longer alone. I didn't have to do anything or everything by myself any longer.

Although, I never thought of myself as a mediocre person, employee, boss or business owner, I certainly recognized that if I was going to empower others, my staff for example, I was going to have to be the best damn leader there was. I no longer allowed myself to be mediocre in any way, shape or form. I decided early in my new career that I was going to provide the best place of employment for my staff and I was going to give of myself every chance I had.

The co-workers who were scared or intimidated by me in my past were no longer a concern of mine. That selfish, self-centered me quickly disappeared and I started helping others shine. I had lived too long with what I thought was a stamp on my forehead saying, "WARNING: DOMINANT PERSONALITY" that I was determined not to treat my staff in that way.

Gratitude, giving and sharing are something we all know we should do. Knowing and doing are two different things. There are many things we do in life that we know we should do differently, but we just don't do them. Smokers know they shouldn't smoke, but they do it anyway. Liars know they shouldn't lie, but they can't bring themselves to tell the truth.

There are thousands of books written with the same content as mine, written in a different way with different stories. Why is it that people still choose to know but not do? It's for the same reasons I only concentrated on money for the longest time rather than giving of myself, sharing and creating. I didn't realize my potential. I wasn't ready to hear it. My paradigms, my beliefs, were too strong for me to be open to new ways.

Did you know that most mentors have mentors of their own? They know the benefit behind it. They know the importance of being accountable to someone else. They also know how easy it is to get sidetracked. It all comes back to keeping your momentum going. Don't just do it one day and not the next. Be consistent. Be honest with yourself.

I have three mentors and one accountability partner. I suggest you start looking for a mentor today. You don't necessarily need three. Start with one, but make sure the one you choose will give you the sense of increase you deserve. Look for a mentor who shines in his or her own life. Remember, you get what you pay for. I choose to RISE ABOVE, so I choose the best of the best. My mentors don't live in my city; in fact, they live in Toronto, Ottawa, Scottsdale, Arizona and Chicago. All I have to do is pick up the phone, dial their number, text them, email, Facebook them, Skype them, messenger them and so on. This modern world allows you to reach out to people millions of miles away from you as if they were with you in your own home.

The only way to stay on track is to make yourself accountable to yourself and others. I have an accountability partner who lives in Chicago. Every Sunday, we send each other an email detailing what we accomplished the previous week and expressing what we want to accomplish for the week that follows. It helps to keep me on track and if I find myself procrastinating or not achieving the results that I wanted, she will catch it and point that out to me. I do the same for her. We boost each other up when it's deserved and we talk to each other when we are experiencing challenges.

With a mentor by your side, you will be able to stay on track even when life throws rocks at you. Your kids, your community and your staff will see you shine and they will admire you for who you are. Lead yourself first. Learn from anyone and everyone and remember, if you say you can't afford a mentor, I say you can't afford not to have one. This is probably the most important first decision you must make.

CHAPTER 9

Your Environment

Let's get right to the point. The environment you provide to others at home, at school and at work is completely dependent on your attitude.

I refer to it as the "environment YOU provide" because you are in total control of how you feel and make others feel around you.

There are certain habits that you can start implementing every day that will change how you perceive yourself and how others see you. But before I get to that, let's think about this for a second.

"A person doesn't get his or her attitude because of his position, a person gets his position because of his or her attitude" – Earl Nightingale. If you're looking to earn a new position in your job, I recommend you pay close attention to this chapter.

Because I provide employment to others, I'm always alert and aware of what's going on around me in the sense that I pay close attention to the individuals that I employ and how they approach life in general. I watch carefully how they interact with their co-workers and I mostly look at who would be a great fit for other positions or even promotions.

Now, let's not kid ourselves. We all have our days and our moments. Things don't always go as planned and it can frustrate us, irritate us and even anger us. How you chose to handle those situations can make a big difference in your present circumstances and your future self. Especially when others, like your employer, have somewhat of a say in what your future may hold for you. I experience those moments as well. I haven't always provided the best environment around me, but I make a conscious effort to consistently work on myself to improve the environment I share with others.

Let's start with a simple gesture that is easy to apply and turn into a new habit. These ideas I'm sharing can be implemented in any environment. I can't see what you do every day or whom you deal with, if you work from home or in a corporate office. I don't know if you're a student, a stay-at-home mom, a janitor, a driver, a manager or an entrepreneur. So, I'm going to share my views from an office standpoint and as a business owner. It's up to you to choose how or with whom you will apply them.

SAY GOOD MORNING and mean it: The easiest thing you can do when you get into work every morning is say, "good morning" to everyone. Aside from saying good morning to my husband as we wake up each day, I'd dare say that the first "good morning" that comes out of my mouth is as soon as I get out of my car. My garage staff are usually bouncing around somewhere in the yard. Then, within 20 seconds of going through the office door, you will hear another good morning. I make my way through the office and If I don't hear someone say it back to me, I will repeat it and look straight at them until I hear them say it back.

My workplace is basically a house converted into an office, so we have a 2-story building. My office is on the second floor. I make my way up the stairs and as soon as I get to the 2nd level, I look at each person individually sitting at their own desk and say good morning to each one. It's that simple. It doesn't matter if I'm having a great morning or not; I still choose to say good morning in a manner that is optimistic and sets the tone for the rest of the day. I find it depressing and disrespectful to see someone come to work each morning with their head down without acknowledging anyone around them. You may not be a morning person, but I don't really care. If we are going to spend the next eight hours together, we may as well start it off on the right foot.

CHAT FOR A FEW MINUTES: I usually make myself a coffee as soon as I get in. I make my way toward the dispatch room and I start asking questions. Sometimes, it's about how their weekend went and other times, it's straight to the point about what's happening in their department. This is one way for me to get to know my staff first and secondly, if there are issues, I usually hear about it right away. I then know if something needs my immediate attention. I never know unless I ask. My team is pretty good at sharing what's happening, but if I wait too long to ask, I may get my information a bit too late to react at the right time or make a decision when it's necessary.

I proceed in this manner with each department. My bookkeeper usually picks up the mail every morning on her way to work, so I sit with her while I'm having my coffee. We make small talk while I open the mail and we get right into financial discussion if necessary. Again, I usually know within minutes if I have issues I need to deal with during the day. I proceed this way with my GM and my Admin until I finally reach my desk. There are days when I don't make it to my desk until halfway through the day because of things that need to be dealt with, but this approach allows me to provide the leadership that my staff needs.

HAVE FUN and LAUGH: Laughter is also something that you should implement into your daily routine. There are days where we laugh a lot. We joke, tease each other, share stories and we communicate in a way that pumps each other up. If someone is having personal issues, we allow them to talk about it if they choose, sometimes in groups and sometimes one on one and we do our best to laugh about any situation that person is experiencing. But we always manage to get the work done while having fun. I'm serious when I say, you need to have fun. You need to bring laughter into the workplace.

I want to know my staff; I want to know what they like and dislike. When I show interest in them, they open up to me and it allows me to see them for who they truly are, human beings. Life shouldn't just be about work or stress. Joy and love are meant to be shared and experienced by all, no matter the position.

Early after my transition, a comment was made to me by my book-keeper's husband. This is what he said, "I hear you bring life to the office". That was probably one of the best compliments anyone could have given me. First, because it meant my staff noticed that I allowed them to be themselves and have fun and second, because for the first time in a very long time, I felt like I was truly accepted by others and appreciated for who I really was. Let your staff, your department or even your kids bring life to your environment. Laughter is a great remedy for any stressful situation.

Now don't be fooled as there are limits and my staff know that work still needs to get done. I've also learned to balance being nice and being firm. I must be firm from time to time. I'm there to provide structure and give my staff the tools they require to do their job well, but if someone is slacking off or being "mediocre", I immediately tackle it.

OPEN DOOR: For years, we have been accustomed to businesses being run behind closed doors. This modern world can no longer operate in that manner. Employees need to know what's going on if you want them to do their jobs effectively and productively. They will never be able to shine if you hide things from them. Share with them the reason behind changes that are happening and explain why decisions are made along the way. They will respect you much more when you provide a transparent environment with an open-door policy. Don't say you offer an "open-door policy" if your door is always shut. That's not an open-door policy and it's certainly not a transparent environment. How does anyone expect to be involved in day-to-day operations with a door that's always shut?

I don't allow doors to be shut in my office unless someone is in a meeting. There is simply no reason for it. You can walk into my office at any time of the day. You can sit in the chair and I will stop whatever I'm doing to listen to you. That's how I choose to be. I allow people to share and talk about whatever they want and from time to time, I share something about myself. This strategy creates a very comfortable environment if it's done with respect. There are also days when laughter is the last thing on our minds. Stress is sometimes felt throughout the office. We deal with what must be dealt with, with as much positivity as possible and we move on. Our environment is so real that we often joke around that we should have a reality show based on our day-to-day interactions at the office.

BE VULNERABLE: Vulnerability is trusting. It's honesty, courage and being truthful. It's the opposite of weakness. We live in a world where people fear being shamed and judged. Social media may allow us to see the world as a much smaller place, but it also creates more introverted human beings, more mental illness and more ridicule. We may be able to help others in distress by accepting them for who they are.

Having the right attitude means that you own up to whatever has happened. I'd like to say mistakes, but there are no mistakes in life. Choose to be responsible for your actions; if you make a bad decision, own up to it. You will often hear me say to my staff something like "I take full responsibility" or "I'm partly to blame because I didn't give you enough information" or "I'm sorry, it's my fault". I want people around me to be honest. If you show vulnerability, more often than not, you will earn the respect of others.

WHAT YOU SAY MATTERS: Pay attention to the words you use from time to time. Do you typically answer the phone and say to the person on the other end, "**oh you know, it's your typical Monday morning**"? Oh my gosh, I really dislike that! That's how you set the tone for the day and the week ahead of you. You don't want your customer to know that you don't feel like being at work. That's a big no-no and honestly, if you don't like going to work every Monday or if you don't like the environment, it's up to you to change it or maybe it's time to look for another job. I don't want my customers to hear that sort of comment. We survive on customers. What are we thinking? And I certainly don't like to hear it when someone says it to me. It relates a negative image of the environment you work in. It gives the feeling that you hate working and you would rather be somewhere else or be doing something else than serving me at that particular moment. Be conscious of your words and thoughts at all time. It's a "**Great Monday morning**" is much more appreciated by all.

Another big NO-NO for me is when people use the term **ASAP**. It shows a lack of respect for the other person. It's as if you're saying, "I don't care what you're up to or what you're working on, but I'm more important than you." This especially irritates me when it's used with a customer or among co-workers. Whatever happened to **please and thank you? Or at your earliest convenience? Or when it's convenient for you?** You can still state the fact that it is something of high priority without the pressure of making someone drop everything they are doing because you need it ASAP.

My opinion on using this term "ASAP" is that our customer has every right to use the term if we are not doing our job or not providing the service they are paying for, but at no time are we to use it toward a customer as if they need to do something for us. NEVER.

It's all about adjusting your attitude and putting a positive twist on everything you do.

That's the environment I want to create around me, not only for the wellbeing of the people who are in my environment but also for my own wellbeing. Smile, say good morning, chat with others, be positive, use the right words and your day, your week, your month and your year will be full of great stories and events that you will remember forever. You just never know who's watching!

CHAPTER 10

Best of the Best – Cream of the Crop

If you really want to stand out from the crowd, treat your employees as if they are your most important asset. In fact, your employees are your most important customer. If you don't have employees, apply this same concept with your co-workers, the other students in your class or your kids at home. The concept is easily adjustable to your life.

Richard Branson has a number of quotes about employees. I especially like this one:

"Clients do not come first, employees come first. If you take care of your employees, they will take care of the clients."

The organizations that implement this in their workplace usually stand out from the rest. It's usually easy to tell that they are doing something right. There are other entrepreneurs who just can't grasp the idea of giving more to others than what they have themselves and they continue to struggle and can never put their finger on the problem.

I have made a conscious effort over the last few years to really concentrate on my employees, their wellbeing and their growth.

When you walk around my office, you will have a difficult time going around without a smile on your face. WHY? Because I wrote "SMILE" with red lipstick on every mirror, on every whiteboard in each and everyone's office. Even on the microwave door! While using the bathroom, you will see the word "smile" in the mirror in front of you. When you walk in the front door, you will see a positive quote of the week written on a whiteboard. When you're at the reception desk, you will see a sign that says, "go team go" and if you happen to go into the driver's room, you will see a sign that says, "my boss thinks I'm a big deal".

Recently, one of my dispatchers brought two of his five kids to the office. It was my first meet and greet with them. His boy Miguel is ten and his daughter Alexia is eight. Alexia walked into my office with a smile on her face and the conversation proceeded like this:

Alexia: "You like to smile"!

Me: "How can you tell?"

Alexia: "You have the word 'smile" written everywhere".

Me: "It's fun, isn't it? Don't you just feel like smiling when you walk in?" Of course, she said yes, so the entire conversation between us proceeded with a smile.

She and her brother were at the office for maybe an hour. In that one hour, Alexia found one room in the entire building where I had forgotten to write the word "smile". It was in the boardroom. I have no idea how I forgot about it, but she quickly took care of it for me. She took it upon herself to write "smile" on a piece of paper and set it on the shelf so that it would be present at each staff meeting going forward. I truly believe that I forgot about the boardroom because it was meant for her to witness and appreciate the meaning behind it. I hope that I made a difference in her world by choosing to smile and I hope that she pays it forward in everything she does.

I've witnessed this with many people who walk into my office. Other kids have come for visits and I've noticed new things written on whiteboards that were never there before. My other dispatcher's teenage daughter, Emma, was in one day and wrote, "Dad, if you're not smiling, you're doing something wrong!" And that phrase remains on his whiteboard to this day.

Positive affirmations and positive talk will do wonders. You will often hear me use the following words to my staff especially when it's a message geared toward team efforts. "You are the best of the best, cream of the crop". What do you think that says to them? It says, I believe in them, I trust them, I think they are awesome! I always liked this phrase and I remember the first time I heard it. My husband and I had just started dating and were visiting my parents. A family friend happened to stop by and I, of course, proceeded to introduce him to my new boyfriend. The gentleman looked at him and said, "You're with a Beaupré, the best of the best, cream of the crop". I thought that was the best compliment geared toward my family and to myself. I never forgot it and I want my staff to feel that same feeling I had.

The first part of this book was mostly dedicated to you as an individual. You are important and you need to practice positive self-talk and conquer all fears and self-sabotage. It becomes a lot easier for you to do this when you apply what you have learned to everyone around you. You will become a leader.

When you want something for yourself, you should want it for the rest of the world. It doesn't matter if others are difficult to get along with or if you think they are hateful. Just continue to be your best self possible.

I think that investing time in employees is the key to success. The more I learn, the more I want to share with them. I usually gather them up in two separate groups on a weekly basis. I can't do it with my drivers as they are always on the road, but the rest of the staff get time away from their desks to work on their personal growth. In fact, it's a requirement in my office. I share what I learn with them. We usually do a session from Bob Proctor, we follow the session with a discussion and we come up with ways to apply it on a personal level and on a business level. Take goals for example. Already ATTAINED goals, MEDIOCRE goals and "WHEN PIGS FLY" type goals have been explained and put into practice. I went through the same exercise with them as I did with you in this book. Each one of them has learned how to find the "when pigs fly" goal and together as a team, we established some pretty amazing company goals as well.

You're probably thinking, "we're too busy for that" or "I can't afford to take my employees away from their desk. There's work to be done". You're never too busy for personal growth and in this case business growth as well. Investing in your employees is crucial. Make the time! Show them that you respect them enough to allow them to learn new habits, new creative ideas and to want good things for themselves.

It's a proven fact that employees leave their job because of their leader rather than not being happy with the position they hold. If you only employ people for doing a job, they will always just work for money. I often get called "Mom" or "Boss Lady" and I'm okay with that. We have fun with "Mom". I know they call me Mom because they respect me. They know I'm looking after their best interest. It's a great feeling.

They will stay if they feel appreciated and respected and they will stay if they feel they make an impact on the business. They are looking for value, vision, inspiration, authenticity. They are motivated by praise, attention from their leader, opportunity for growth and a sense of increase toward their salary and their future. It's your job to provide it for them. There's no need to spend thousands of dollars on consultants who will tell you what motivates your employees. You can do this yourself; invest in them, talk to them and the answers will come fairly easy.

People who motivate people are what I'm looking for. I want more leaders, not followers. It's not right to think that your receptionist will always be a receptionist or that your janitor has nothing else to offer than to clean one bathroom stall after another. They have so much more to offer if you allow them to participate. Just think about how many people your receptionist talks to in the run of a day. Do you not think she hears the customers' concerns or feedback? She probably has ideas on how to make certain tasks more efficient for each person in the company. She probably has ideas on how to promote the company to the customers. Tap into her ideas. Let her know you're interested in knowing more. Your janitor probably overhears many complaints from the staff during the course of a day. He probably has insight that you don't have. He probably has ideas to resolve internal issues that you never thought of. Tap into his ideas and thoughts as well. Both employees may have enough knowledge and skills to make you millions of dollars if you let them. Allow them to share that with you. Even if she's the best receptionist you have ever had, she'll be great at training a replacement for her job and move on to a higher position within the company. The possibilities are endless, they really are, and you will only start seeing a difference in your business once you recognize this.

I involve my staff in just about everything that goes on in my business. I hardly make decisions without talking with them first. It would be wrong of me to make decisions without getting the facts I need or getting opinions from those who actually do the work. They know best. They certainly know better than me most times, because I'm in the background. I'm providing a vision for them. I don't do the work they do day in and day out. If I don't involve them or get their opinions, I could make really bad decisions on behalf of the company. I encourage participation. I challenge them to get involved. My job is to show them the way, the future I envision for the company. I show them the values my husband and I stand by. I provide the tools they need to be more efficient because I listen to them. You'll often hear my staff say that whenever they ask for something, they usually received it yesterday because I don't procrastinate. I get it done and it shows that I care about them.

I want employees who desire to take over my role in the future. I want employees who make decisions according to my values even when I'm not there. I want employees to tell me when I'm off course or when I'm not following my own advice. I want them to believe that there is so much more to life than settling for what they currently have.

I know that there is a risk in me helping them grow. I know that they could suddenly desire more for themselves and find a better employer who will offer it to them. I know that I risk losing really awesome people by expanding their mind, but I also know that if I continue to offer them growth and to be open to their ideas, they will grow with me. If for some reason, they feel that I can no longer offer any more opportunities for them, then I still succeeded. I showed them the way to more, to better, to a brighter future for themselves. If I were to operate in fear of losing them, in fear of them becoming better individuals, I would never expand and grow myself. It's all about giving and helping others. If they stay with you, that's fantastic; if they leave, then they had a reason to. It's a risk I'm willing to take. I know by providing more education, more knowledge will come. It's my job to make it worth their while. It's my job to continue to grow along with them.

Happy employees will always be your biggest asset. They will, in turn, make your customers happy. How I treat them is how they will treat my customers. They become more productive, the morale increases and it shows in everything they do. I continue to show them that they make a difference and they continue to show me that they ARE the difference.

Small ideas can sometimes result in big positive changes. A while back, I was struggling to come up with a new idea to reach out to new customers. What did I do? I turned it over to my staff for their input. Together, we came up with a way that our drivers could interact more with the customers by offering the customer a 10% discount on their next service. How did we accomplish this? We gave each driver a business card. Each one is numbered and has an empty space for a name. The driver writes his name on the card, hands it over to the customer and explains that the next time they require our services, they should call the main office; all they have to do is reference the number on the card and the name of the driver and the company will give them 10% off.

The challenge at the time was how to get the drivers to take the time to do this. Their time on the road is precious and they must get from point A to point B within schedule. Together, we were able to come up with a plan to give each driver a $25 gift card of their choice for every customer who used the discount card with their name on it. This idea may seem small to some and to others, it may be overwhelming, but I can honestly say that it was welcomed by all employees and we still apply it today.

The drivers motivate each other and congratulate each other every time a customer uses a 10% discount card. It keeps them wanting to be involved knowing they make a difference by bringing more customers forward. It's simple but effective and best of all, the staff created this idea. It motivates them to think of more ideas and to share them with the rest of the team and together, we continue to grow.

This example shows us that we as a team work toward:

1) "Giving a sense of increase to our customers" by offering a discount card.

2) It then shows that we offer a "sense of increase" to our drivers by compensating them for their efforts.

3) It proves that we do not worry about our competition. In fact, we create our own work by offering our customers something no one else is offering.

4) It shows we offer growth within the company. It proves that we want the best for others as we do for ourselves by offering compensation.

5) It proves to the customer that we are grateful for their business.

6) And we are grateful to our employees as evidenced by recognition.

Work toward a common goal. Never settle for less than what you expect. If you expect excellence, don't tolerate mediocrity. Raise your standards. Your employees, your kids, your spouse and your customers will respect you and will always return for more.

Decisions will become so much easier to make. Problems will come and go but will not seem to affect you as much as they used to because you are now tackling them as a team.

Choose to trust others until they prove you wrong. Believe me when I say, once you can give without fear of any kind, you will rise above all.

My standard is that I employ the "best of the best, cream of the crop human beings". I feel it in my gut and I believe it every day. I tell my employees how I see them; therefore, it is reality.

CHAPTER 11

NOURISH Your Team

It is so easy to recognize if a group of people work as a team or not by simply observing how they interact with each other when they are all gathered together. Think about all your company events or staff parties that you may have been part of in the past and remember how people mingled. Did they mingle in groups according to their departments or industry? Or did they all mix together, no matter their job titles, position or department? I know I've been to many gatherings where I didn't feel comfortable at all if I tried to fit in a group that I was not compatible with or if I didn't do the same type of work as they did. Stories and jokes are going around, but you don't get any of it. Or better yet, they try to include you, but you really had to be there to fully experience the story. Does any of this sound familiar?

Here's another example that's easy to tell a non-team environment when you're at work and the only conversations going around the lunchroom are about how bad the managers are or how poorly you've been treated over the past week. I remember back to my job in the insurance business; every lunch hour, employees from different departments would gather in the employee lounge and all you could hear was negative comments, which would almost turn into a contest of who had the worst boss. This would go on hour after hour, day after day.

Better yet, have you ever been to a business establishment, let's say a grocery store, retail store, hair salon, hospital or restaurant and overheard the employees negatively engaging in conversations about their boss or the atmosphere of their office in front of you, or better yet, while serving you? It happens so often and they're not even conscious of what they are doing.

If you employ people, this should be one of your biggest concerns. How your employees represent you or your company when you're not looking is crucial. And, if you're an employee, you should really make a conscious effort to notice what you are sharing with others. Now, I know that we can never stop gossip and drama, but it's up to us as employees, employers and leaders to do the best we can to control this sort of behavior. Your career, the success of your business and your lifestyle depend on it.

What I noticed in my transport business is that I had a diverse group of employees who from time to time would disrespect each other because they simply didn't understand the value that each department brought to the table. Drivers are on the road and do very physical work while office staff need to put the plans together, the structure, the policies and so on. Each group bring values to the table and what most employees tend to forget is that we need each one of them for the day-to-day operations of any business. The drivers can't do their jobs if there is no office staff and the office staff won't have a job if there are no drivers to deliver the product or service.

How do we bring these people together and create a team environment? It's much easier than you think. I decided early on in my transition to the trucking business that I would provide the best place of work possible and that I would create a team environment where everyone respected each other, no matter what job or position they had. You can have the best of the best for employees, but if you don't look after them or want the best for them, they will certainly not represent you the way you would like them to. Just think about the conversations you take part in on a daily basis. Do you tend to put a positive twist to your conversation or are you easily influenced by what others are saying? Remember what I said about self-sabotage. Talking is overrated and unless you bring value to the other person you are speaking to, you should not be speaking at all. If you can recognize this in yourself, you should be able to recognize how easy it is for everyone around you to fall into the same trap.

My wish for you is that you can become very aware of your surroundings and the people around you. I wish for you to be able to tell the difference between good and bad apples. When we shop for apples at the grocery store, we usually leave the rotten ones behind. It's important to bring this concept to the workplace or even our social life. The only way to recognize the good or bad apples is by interacting with them and really listen to what's happening rather than just hearing noise around us.

Looking after and wanting the best for your employees means you nourish them with knowledge, with opportunities, training, recognition, praise, gratitude, money and so on. Nourish is the most important word in the above phrase. We all know that nourishment is necessary for growth. You need food to survive. The same applies to your environment in your personal life and your workplace. Whatever you feed the people around you will determine its effectiveness and survival for a company of any size.

Let's explore this in detail:

Nourish them with your VISION: Where do you want your business to go in the future? Whether you plan to expand the business or remain the same, it's important to share that vision. If you expect a certain level of professionalism from them, then they need to know. Share all the details you can with your team. If the team knows where you're headed, it's easier for them to decide if they want to join you on that journey. If you don't want any bad apples in the team, they need to know that it's not accepted. Those who don't like your vision will always have issues and will eventually move on to other things on their own or you will send them on their way. Make peace with this right away; it's okay to let some people go. It's best to sacrifice the work until you find yourself the best team to do the work. Then you're on the right track.

Frame your vision and mission statement and post it on the wall. Make it visible for everyone to see around the office.

Nourish them with GOALS: You can't expect your team to work toward a goal if you don't have a clear one yourself. Everyone deserves to feel that they are working toward something bigger and better.

Your vision will come easy if you have solid goals. If you are still unsure how to set proper goals, refer to the chapter "when pigs fly". Once your goals are clear, record yourself reading them and share them with the members of your staff you think will benefit from it, especially those you include in personal growth meetings. The concept behind the "Power Life Script" is to write down everything you want your life to be or your business to be in the future. The trick is to write it in the positive tense as if it's already happening. If it's clear and precise, it will give the staff a reason to come to work every day knowing they have something to look forward to.

A good way to set big goals for the business is by bringing everyone together and allowing them to brainstorm. This will allow you to see each person's character, the limits they set for themselves and where you need to put more effort going forward. Allowing them to dream of bigger and better things means that it's now your responsibility to nourish those goals of theirs and provide opportunities for them to grow into. Just because they have goals does not mean they will leave. They will stay if they see you really care about their growth as individuals.

Nourish them with COMMUNICATION: Communication is key. Let's do our best never to assume that someone understands what we are trying to accomplish or why. Never assume that someone has a clear picture of what you expect of them. Assuming can be costly. It's more important to gather facts in order to make proper decisions. Include your team in decision making; explain, teach and show them the way. If you TELL rather than SHOW, you will never get the results you are aiming for. Telling is not a leadership skill; showing is. The result is that your staff will feel great when they've accomplished the task at hand correctly the first time around or if they feel comfortable asking questions because the lines of communications are open. Transparency is what you're aiming for. Just because you know how to do something or just because you think the other person is smart enough to figure it out doesn't mean they are or will. Time is valuable. Showing someone how to do something right the first time around will allow you additional time to concentrate on other goals much faster. It's best to share your knowledge and help them grow.

Nourish them with RESPECT: Please and thank you go a long way. Acknowledging difficulties and allowing them to share them with you is even better. Everyone wants to be treated like a human being. Allow them to make human errors but respect them enough to show you care by interacting with them in the sense that you are there to help them. Respect goes a long way and it will come back to you tenfold. When you show your staff respect, they will do just about anything for you and it should go both ways. If they need something from you, make sure you make yourself available. If you promise them something, make sure you come true on your promise. If they depend on you, make sure you show up. If an obstacle comes along and a bad decision was made, regroup, ask questions and come up with the root cause that everyone takes responsibility for.

Nourish them with SOLUTIONS: A leader's job is to provide the right tools to make everyone's daily tasks easier and efficient. For example, a newer computer, an ergonomic chair or an efficient software. If tools are not provided and struggles continue to arise repeatedly, employees will most likely remain unhappy. It's best to aim at solving problems yesterday. That is my approach. I analyze the situation and go to work to solve it. Some situations or issues are easier solved than others, but if communication is present by explaining the reason behind the delay, at least my employees will respect the fact that I am still trying to reach the result they would like to see. Here's an example: transport trucks are expensive to purchase. If one needs to be replaced because of its age and ever-growing cost of repairs continue to climb, then a purchase would probably need to be made. These are not always easy purchases and can take time to accomplish. It's important that I share with the team that the goal is to purchase a newer truck when the funds are available.

Don't forget that you can't solve a problem if you don't have all the facts, so ask questions. I don't pretend to know everything; in fact, my team knows more than I do. There is no way for me to be able to do everyone's job, therefore, I count on them to inform me of the issues they are having. If things drag on and I find out something wasn't going well for quite some time, they understand that they must take responsibility for not having shared it with me. Always put yourself in their shoes, open your mind to change, open your eyes to doing things in new ways. The world is changing fast and I don't want you to miss anything along the way. There is no better way than to include your team in your problem solving. They will feel like they make a difference and they should BE the difference.

Nourish them with RECOGNITION: This is so, so, so important! A respected and recognized employee will stay with you and be loyal to you forever if you do it right. Find a way to recognize your team in front of their peers. Include them in the team success if they had a part to play in it. Everyone wants to feel loved and appreciated. Remember, we all want to live a life of abundance. More love, more appreciation, more respect, more goals, more, more and more of everything is what they are looking for.

About a year ago, I visualized an app that employees could access at least once a day for important memos, for recognition for doing acts of kindness, for recognizing each other, for earning points that would then turn into bonuses for them. I really disliked going over the payroll each Monday knowing that I may have missed something one of them did the week before that may have deserved recognition.

I wanted so much for them to know that every little thing they do or go out of their way to do for the company was appreciated. I have no way of knowing everything that goes on in the run of a day especially when I have drivers on the road thousands of miles away from the office. I could see this app filling that gap; I could see them sharing stories, just like social media, but for the company employees only. If a driver had a clean inspection at a DOT scale, for example, then he would earn 250 points, which would result in $25 toward whatever he/she wanted. If someone really went out of their way to do something special, they would get a "TY" thank you message worth 5 points, or "IM" for Impressive worth 50 points along with a little blurb telling the rest of the team what he or she had accomplished or gone out of his or her way to do. Rather than concentrating on just a few employees who tend to always stand out from the rest, I wanted all of them to feel equally important. The hope was also that the camaraderie from office staff and drivers would become more positive and they would be able to see how important each person is in their own role. The results were and still are astonishing.

Every day, I see drivers thanking someone from the office for a favor or a job well done. I see drivers helping each other when they meet up on the road. They buy each other lunch or coffee. I see admiration and respect within the company that I was so hoping for and I was able to make it come to life. I've had employees who have earned enough points to pay for trips to Las Vegas, bought a washer and dryer, kayaks or groceries for the family rather than using the money from their paycheck, gas gift cards and so on. I can't even begin to share how much of an impact this little app has made in my business.

I want all my employees going home at the end of the day feeling as though they accomplished something fabulous that day and every day. I want them to know they make a difference in my life, in my world, in the world of each team member they work with day in and day out. I want them to feel a sense of accomplishment and to feel equal to everyone else.

Nourish them with GIFTS: Gifts don't have to be big. A gift can be a box of doughnuts for the team. It can be a gift certificate of some sort. Don't treat everything your employees do as a regular part of their job. Yes, they all have a job to do. We all do. But everyone wants to know that the little things matter. Never approach it on terms of "that's what your job is" or "that's what you're supposed to do". There are so many people who do extra every day and even if they do what they are supposed to do, if they do it extra well, recognize them and do something special for them. I've seen myself give a $25 gift card to a driver because a friend of mine said he smiled at her while she passed him on the highway. How awesome is that? I give out gifts when positive feedback is given from another co-worker or a customer. I give them gifts for such little things that you would probably laugh at me. But I know that I'm making my staff feel special and the more they know I notice the little things they do, the more things they want to do. It's that simple. Giving is a big part of growing a team and it's a big part of our everyday lives.

Throw staff parties for them and pay for everything. I know some business owners don't give anything at Christmas time to any of their staff. That really hurts me. Employees work so hard all year. They deserve to be celebrated at least once a year, if not more. My Christmas parties are so much fun and I usually get 100% participation. I make sure no one leaves empty handed. Even the spouses leave with some sort of a gift. This is the one evening of the year where I want them to let their guard down, enjoy each other's company, share stories and know that the owners appreciate them so very much. I feel great about doing it for them and I know they appreciate it.

Never give and expect something in return. Give from your heart. Don't say that you can't afford it. If you're buying yourself a coffee every morning, I know you can probably afford to buy one more for the person behind you or for someone at work. Giving doesn't have to be huge or monetary, but it must be part of your daily routine. If you don't understand the concept or the value behind it or if you're always afraid to give because you're afraid it's taking away from you, then it's something you definitely need to start working extra hard at. If you continue to think of lack of money or lack of resources, you will continue to get the same. Change that thinking process to: the more you give for little things, the more you will receive in return and the more you will flourish in your personal life and in business because they will continue to give you more of themselves

Nourish them with TRUST: Allow people to learn the hard way. Let them make mishaps. If you always try to prevent your employees from making a human error, they will never grow or learn. It's going to happen at some point or another. Let them show you what they can do and from there, tweak it if you feel they need guidance, but approach it with respect and acknowledge when they do some things well. Remember that there are no mistakes in life. It may be an obstacle rather than a mistake, but again, obstacles usually occur in order to slow us down so we can evaluate the direction we are going in.

There is always a positive way to look at things. Nothing ever HAPPENS TO YOU; they just happen because they were meant to happen. No one is put on this planet to suffer, so you are not chosen among others to be the bearer of bad luck or the only person who must suffer. Trust others and trust the Universe that it always has your back, no matter what. Whenever I sense that someone is going through a challenge or is unsure of themselves, I always reinforce it by saying, "you've got this", "I know you'll do the right thing", "I trust you". Those words go a long way. I may have the same concerns as they do, but I can never let them see me sweat; otherwise, we'll never accomplish anything. If the result wasn't as we had hoped for, I need to appreciate the effort and understand that I gave them the confidence to at least give it their best shot.

Nourish them with HUMILITY: AHHH, this is a good one. Humility according to the *Cambridge English Dictionary* is "the quality of not being proud because you are aware of your bad qualities".

Your job may come with a special title and that's great; however, remember that we are all equal. The title doesn't make you who you are. Your attitude does. Whether you're older, have more education than others or even make more money than others, it changes nothing. Being down to earth is what will make you stand out. If everyone hates seeing you come around, I'd say you need to adjust your attitude or your approach to them. Human beings were all created the same, no matter the race, religion, age or title.

When I look back at my years in real estate, I shake my head at myself for who I was then – self-centered, ego driven and greedy – and it really didn't bring me any more happiness. In fact, it isolated me from society. Now, I approach life with a totally different outlook and it's all about making others feel special. I can honestly tell you my life feels a lot more rewarding and fulfilled than it ever did. Laugh at yourself in front of others, share your embarrassing stories, take responsibility for your actions, be responsible and admit when you're wrong. "That's my fault" is always respected.

Nourish them with HONESTY: Honesty is always the best policy in any situation. Be honest with yourself, with your team and with your customers. I know I can tell when someone is pulling a fast one on me. I can tell when they don't want to admit they did something wrong or won't take responsibility for their actions. Can you?

I ask my team to always do the right thing and everything will work out in the end. A customer will invariably appreciate knowing the truth rather than hearing a long-winded false story. If a mishap happened, so be it. Mishaps or human errors do occur and again, they occurred for a reason.

Don't wait until it's too late to approach someone because they are not living up to your expectations. Be honest about what is expected, but do it in a way that they know you are helping them grow. Positive or negative feedback is still better than no feedback.

Nourish them with EDUCATION: There should never be a price tag on education. None for yourself and none for your team. I recently did a workshop on leadership to business executives. I had a woman in the class who was the CFO of her company. She shared a story with me about how her past employer never allowed her out of the office because he was afraid to lose her to his competition. She was never allowed out to conventions, seminars, courses or anything, for that matter. In the end, the result was exactly what he was afraid of, which was he lost her to someone else. See, he knew she was smart, but he wanted her to remain a secret. He did not work at creating all the opportunities for her to grow alongside him. He had a fear that she would gain more knowledge and maybe outsmart him. Our job as leaders is to create opportunities for others, to empower them and to lead the way to a better way of living. Her boss was lacking his own knowledge on leadership.

I know that I can't be everywhere all at once. I can't attend every seminar or every meeting. I employ people to represent me and my company. I employ them to learn more and to bring it back to me with new ideas, so we can grow even more. I encourage education. This world is full of information. I would rather tap into the knowledge of 100 people anytime rather than depend solely on my own. Put a group of people together and you can accomplish many great things. Put only one person on a task and he or she may encounter many defeats to the point that nothing is accomplished.

Nourish them with CREATIVITY: With knowledge comes creativity. Everything we use on a daily basis was created by someone. Someone had to have the idea of creating the wheel, the chair, the cell phone, the computer and it goes on and on. Your employees are full of creative ideas. You just have to find a way to let them express them and allow them that freedom. Call an office meeting, bring them together and brainstorm ideas. You'll never see a better way if you always depend on your own knowledge and creativity. If you think your receptionist is only a receptionist and nothing more, you could be missing out on some big opportunities. It's your job as a leader to bring the best out in them. Don't steal their ideas and don't use them to your benefit. Listen to what they say and explore those ideas. Compensate them for thinking creatively. Praise them or even better, promote them. There are no limits in this world. The only limits are the ones you put on yourself and your team. If you are not allowing creativity, you are acting out of fear. Fear of growth. There is such a thing called "fear of success" and I'd say most of the time, it's the fear of seeing someone else succeed.

I've told my staff repeatedly that my wish for them is that they all make a minimum salary of $100,000/year each. I've even offered them to write their own salary and to approach me with their ideas and what they are willing to do to earn more money. Now it doesn't mean that I give them an instant pay increase. It means, I allow them to create new ways, to want more for themselves and I work with them to make it happen. If they are willing and able and they have a plan in mind, I will do whatever I can to make it happen for them as long as they show me they want it badly enough for themselves.

Nourish with LOVE: I'm in no way referring to romantic love. I'm talking about genuine caring for others. In that same workshop I taught, there was a gentleman who was sharing a story about his company having a summer staff party, but none of the executives showed up to the party. That's not love at all. Nourishing with love means you are showing an interest in others. It's treating others as "people" rather than always "an employee". When you can show others that you truly care for them without it benefiting you, you can say you are nourishing with love. You can learn a lot about people by asking them questions about themselves rather than always talking about yourself. Everyone wants to be heard and feel like they are the most important person in that moment. Do you know anything about their kids? Better yet, do you know the kids' names? Does anyone have special talents or special hobbies? A leader should always be mentally present rather than just be there in physical form.

If they have problems at home or with their health, do everything you can to help them. Allow them paid time off, give them time to recover from whatever has happened and always leave your door open.

Nourish them with **support, cooperation, encouragement, forgiveness, consistency, positivity, time, money…** This could go on forever.

Now you're probably reading this saying, "I already know all of this". And we all do. It's the human way, however, to perceive knowing and doing as two different things. The secret is consistency. Don't just do it once in a while. Do it all the time. That's when you become a true leader. It's when you can put all of these nourishing ideas into practice and it becomes second nature each and every day. Then you are on your way to be a true leader. The benefits will astound you as to what your team, your kids, your spouse and your friends will do when they all come together.

The app that I introduced into the business has brought people closer together. My entire staff now work together rather than against each other. They thank each other and congratulate each other and hardly anything goes unnoticed.

Staff parties are no longer divided into groups according to their job. No more stories that others don't know about. There is no longer daily drama about being treated unfairly because they are recognized for almost everything they do. I don't worry about missing anything anymore. I would never claim to be or to have everything perfect at work or in my personal life, but I do have the best of the best, cream of the crop staff working alongside me every day and I am so proud of all of them.

A great leader is one who makes a difference in people's lives and who finds a creative way to nourish the team. Sort out the bad apples; let them go. Sort out the mediocre employees; you can't force them to work harder or smarter. Only keep the great ones.

It all begins with you, your vision, your goals, and you wanting to give of yourself to others. That's a great leader!

CHAPTER 12

Give a Damn

I've worked with people for years. I've come across all personalities and the secret to making a good connection with people is to always put yourself in their shoes, understand where they are coming from and also adjust your personality to theirs. I'm very conscious of how people think, and I would guess that you may be looking at my approach in business as soft or even weak. Love, compassion and giving are so uncomfortable for the average person, they're often shrugged for that reason – we are terrified of looking weak or soft.

There is nothing delicate about my approach; in fact, I asked my team if they saw me as weak or too soft and the answer was that they saw me as a strong leader, a determined woman, straightforward and honest. I would dare say that they even think I'm strict. I know this because I am very demanding. I show them that I have high expectations for myself and for them. There's a reason behind my way of thinking, which is if we want to keep up with this modern world, we must bring forth our 100% every day. Otherwise, others will take the lead.

Technology and machinery may make our lives easier and give us shortcuts to do our jobs faster, but it will never provide the love, compassion and empathy that human beings require. We go to great extents to educate ourselves on how to operate machines, but we forget to educate ourselves on personal development and living life with intent. Living life with intent means you have a clear plan and a clear "when pigs fly" type of goal. It also means you give a damn about the direction in which you are headed and about the wellbeing of others around you.

We all have a role to play in life, be it at home with our families, at play with friends or at work. At home, we need to give love to our spouses and our kids. With friends we should always give a shoulder to cry on and at work, we should work with passion and intent. It all starts with taking responsibility and being accountable, but most of all, helping and giving of ourselves. Leaders should take this very seriously because a leader's job is to lead by example. The only way to get others to give a damn about what they do, their approach in life and at work is to start with leading in the same manner. If you're a parent, you're a leader. If you are part of a group of some sort, you are still a leader. It makes no difference what title you hold at work. You can still be a leader.

Human beings have feelings and since we know and understand that technology can't replace feelings or provide love, then we need to make an extra effort to put it out there into the world. Love is what humanity craves the most. Why do marriages fail so easily? It's a lack of love, so we go searching for it somewhere else. Why do people leave their jobs? It's not because they don't love the work they do. It's because they lack the love from their leaders. Why is there war in the world? It's still a lack of love! It's a constant battle to fill this need we have to feel special. The world is full of hatred and jealousy. Look around you. Social media is making the world a smaller place, but it's certainly not bringing more love. In fact, it's making society crave it more. We crave the immediate satisfaction of love and the lack of it is causing more mental illnesses, wars and suicides. What is the root cause? Lack of love! Being passionate and loving does not make anyone delicate. It just means you care.

IF we want to be successful, we must start by being valuable to others. I used to just concentrate on money and how much of it I could earn. Of course, I still love making money, but I love helping others even more. We are all unique and we all have something to offer. You will rise above when you lift others. Let's not worry about the other person recognizing or appreciating what we do for them. It doesn't matter.

I made a conscious decision in the past few years to never say, "what's in it for me?" It's not always easy, I'll be the first to admit it, but when I find it difficult, I just remind myself that I am here to help others. That simple. I aim to be someone's cheerleader, confidant, mentor or friend.

This life is a constant journey to growth and recreating who we are to a new and improved version of ourselves. I wouldn't want to be the same person I was at the age of 19 or 29 or 40, for that matter. I'm looking for growth and to be a much better person today than I was yesterday. Don't go back to your comfort zone because others don't understand your journey. It's not for them to understand. Don't try to change anyone but yourself. Don't wait for others to follow you. Those who want to be in your life will follow. Go out and help someone else; make a difference in someone's life.

I love the following quote: "When setting out on a journey, do not seek advice from those who have never left home" – RUMI

I plan to live my life as I wish to live it. I purposely love those whom I choose to love. I plan to go where I want to go because one day, all options and opportunities may be taken away from me and I don't want to live with any regrets. I don't want to say, "I should have, when I had the chance". I respect the life that I've been given, and I live it with intent. I know I am here to help others. I also recognize that I was NOT put on this earth to suffer, be weak or to be poor – nobody is. I am a creator, just like you are, and I plan on using all my faculties to create and give more and more.

Start changing small daily habits, for example, start reading, stimulate your mind, talk to someone you find interesting, do something scary, explore new things and new places, rest when you have to and make sure that you always surround yourself with people who will bring the best out in you. Prove to yourself that you are capable and willing.

Don't try to impress anyone but yourself. Aim to teach and empower. You'll be amazed how productivity and morale will increase. A clear vision equals clarity. When you know where you're headed, things become so much easier and clearer. Planning solves short- and long-term battles. The more proactive you are, the better equipped and ready you are for anything that comes your way. Creativity equals innovation. Explore your talents and gifts. There is a reason you are on this planet and it's certainly not to be a fixture. Willingness means growth. The more open and aware you are, the faster you will grow and achieve amazing goals. I learn from life and other people every day. It has taught me more about myself than any school could have ever done.

Giving a damn will make you stand out from the crowd. Why? Because most people don't! It's that simple. After reading this book, I hope you will have a new outlook on life. I wish for you to live every day purposely, with passion and kindness. Give yourself permission to dream big goals. Stop playing small. You deserve whatever it is you desire.

Show up physically and mentally in everything you do and in every conversation you engage in. Don't get caught up in the self-sabotage we talked about. Be conscious of what you say to yourself and others. Can you imagine what the world would be like if we started being kinder to ourselves and then flooded the world with the same kindness? I believe we would be experiencing much more love all around.

A person who gives a damn can never be defeated by anything or anyone. When you can't be defeated, you become successful.

The abundant life you are seeking is here and now! You're in for a treat, trust me. It's a beautiful, gratifying feeling to RISE ABOVE!

It's time for you to get
MORE OUT OF LIFE

Ambition is the first page toward success

Services For You

Discover how Denise can further help you and your business.

- Executive Coaching
- 1 on 1 Coaching
- Workshops
- Speaking Engagements

You Can Expect...

A unique opportunity to give meaning to your career, business, relationships and your life as a whole.

Equipped with some of the World's most effective leadership tools, you will be able to set and consistently achieve all your individual, team and/or organizational goals.

Why choose Denise?

Using the right Mentor is a proven / cost-effective method to reach your goals. Today, people across all walks of life use coaches to move forward.

www.DeniseBeaupre.com

info@denisebeaupre.com
(506) 381-4218

ABOUT THE AUTHOR

Denise Beaupré is a dynamic leader who motivates and engages her team to work toward company goals. As Owner & COO of Auction Transport, Denise is well versed in the challenges of operating a successful business. Prior to this adventure, Denise excelled for 13 years in real estate, achieving many awards and recognitions along the way for most listings, most sales and highest commission earned, and she was recognized as one of the Top 100 Realtors in North America with her firm. In the trucking industry, she has received recognition for "Employer of Choice" two years in a row and an award for "Women Who Inspire in the Trucking Industry" to a more recent recognition "Growth 500 ranking of Canada's Fastest-Growing Companies" with a 119% growth over a period of five years. Building leaders is her passion, and she provides workshops and yearly mentoring to entrepreneurs and executives who are looking to rise above. In her spare time, she is an abstract artist and enjoys traveling and spending time with family and friends.

Giving a Voice to Creativity!

Wouldn't you love to help the physically, spiritually, and mentally challenged?

Would you like to make a difference in a child's life?

Imagine giving them:
confidence; self-esteem; pride; and self-respect.
Perhaps a legacy that lives on.

You see, that's what we do.
We give a voice to the creativity in their hearts,
for those who would otherwise not be heard.

Join us by going to

HeartstobeHeard.com

Help us, help others.

Made in the USA
San Bernardino, CA
20 November 2018